PYTHON PROGRA
LANGUAGE FOR BEGINNERS

A Crash Course Guide with Tricks and Tools for Your First Approach to Learn and Programming with Python

Clark Wes

contained within this document, including, but not limited to, — errors, omissions, or inaccuracies.

... give a date to a dream and you will have a goal ...

Table of Contents

Introduction

There are plenty of books on this subject on the market, thanks again for choosing this one! Every effort was made to ensure it is full of as much useful information as possible, please enjoy!

Each CPU has its own set of instructions and, consequently, machine code and one of its own assembly languages. A program written for an Intel brand CPU will not work on a CPU designed by another manufacturer, such as Motorola. Even different versions of the same CPU have instruction sets that are not fully compatible with each other: the most evolved models of a CPU family can incorporate instructions that are not found in the older.

If we want a program to run on more than one type of computer, will we have to write it again for each particular CPU? For a long time an attempt was made to define some type of (universal assembly language), that is, a language whose mnemonic codes, not corresponding to those of the machine code of any concrete computer.

As you read further, you will learn more about programming and how vast the universe is.

Chapter 1

Introduction to Computers

1.1. Computers

The dictionary of the Royal Academy defines electronic computer as an electronic, analog or digital machine, equipped with a large capacity memory and methods of information processing, capable of solving mathematical and logical problems through the automatic use of computer programs.

The definition itself gives us indications about some basic elements of the computer: the memory, and some device capable of performing mathematical and logical calculations.

Memory is a great store of information. In memory we store all types of data: numerical values, texts, images, etc. The device responsible for carrying out mathematical and logical operations, which is called the Arithmetic-Logic Unit (UAL), is like a calculator capable of working with that data and producing, from them, new data (the result of operations). Another device is responsible for transporting the information from the memory to the UAL, controlling the UAL to carry out the pertinent operations and depositing the results in the memory: the Control Unit. The set formed by the Control Unit and the UAL is known as the Central Processing Unit (or CPU).

We can imagine the memory as a huge closet with numbered drawers and the CPU as a person who, equipped with a calculator (the UAL), is able to search operands in memory, perform calculations with them and leave the results in memory.

1.2 Coding of the information

We will use a more technical language: each of the (drawers) that make up the memory is called a cell (from memory) and the number that identifies it is its position or address, although sometimes we will use these two terms to refer also to the corresponding cell.

Each memory position allows storing a sequence of ones and zeros of fixed size. Why ones and zeros? Because the current computer technology is based on the simplicity with which it is possible to build binary devices, that is, they can adopt two possible states: on / off, there is current / no current, true / false, one / zero...

Is it possible to represent data as varied as numbers, texts, images, etc. with only ones and zeros? The answer is yes (although with certain limitations). To understand it better, we need to pause briefly to consider how information is represented with binary values.

An encoding associate signs with the elements of a set that we call meanings. In the West, for example, we code numbers from 0 to 9 with the set of signs {0, 1, 2, 3, 4, 5, 6, 7, 8, 9}. In doing so, we match these symbols with quantities, that is, with their meaning: the symbol (6) represents the quantity six. The set of signs does not have to be finite. We can combine the digits in sequences that correspond to, for example, the natural numbers.

The sequence of digits (99) forms a new sign that we associate with the quantity ninety-nine. Computers have only two basic signs, {0, 1}, but they can be combined in sequences, so we are not limited to just two possible meanings.

A variable that can only take one of the two binary values is called the bit acronym for a binary digit. It is usual to work with bit streams of fixed size. An 8-bit sequence is called a byte (although in Spanish the correct term is octet, this is not just imposed and the English voice is used). With a sequence of 8 bits we can represent 256 different meanings. The range [0, 255] of natural values comprises 256 values, so we can represent any of them with an 8-bit pattern. We could decide, in principle, that the correspondence between bytes and natural values is completely arbitrary. Thus, we could decide that the sequence 00010011 represents, for example, the natural number 0 and that the sequence 01010111 represents the value 3. Although this arbitrary association is possible, it is not desirable, since it greatly complicates carry out operations with the values. Adding, for example, would require a table to be memorized to say what is the result of performing the operation with each pair of values, and there are 65536 different pairs!

The positional representation systems of the numbers allow establishing this association between bit sequences and natural numerical values in a systematic way. We focus the discourse on 8-bit sequences, although everything we set out below is valid for sequences of other sizes. The value of a bit string $s\ b_7\ b_6\ b_5\ b_4\ b_3\ b_2\ b_1\ b_0$ is, in a conventional positional system, $P_7\ b_i \cdot 2_i$. Thus, bit sequence 00001011 encodes the value i = 0

$0 \cdot 2_7 + 0 \cdot 2_6 + 0 \cdot 2_5 + 0 \cdot 2_4 + 1 \cdot 2_3 + 0 \cdot 2_2 + 1 \cdot 2_1 + 1 \cdot 2_0 = 8 + 2 + 1 = 11$. The bit from the left it is called ((most significant bit)) and the bit to the right is called (least significant bit).

So far we have seen how to code positive values. Can we also represent negative amounts? The answer is yes. Let's briefly consider three ways to do it. The first is very intuitive: it consists in using the most significant bit to encode the sign; if it is 0, for example, the number expressed with the remaining bits is positive (with the positional representation you already know), and if it is 1, it is negative. For example, the value of 00000010 is 2 and that of 10000010 is −2. Making sums with positive and negative values is relatively complicated if we encode the sign of a number. This major complication also moves to the necessary circuitry. Bad thing.

An alternative way of coding positive and negative quantities is the so-called ((complement to one)). It consists of the following: the positional representation of a number (which must be able to be expressed with 7 bits) is taken and all its bits are inverted if it is negative. The sum of coded numbers thus is relatively simple: the conventional sum is made and, if an overflow has not occurred, the result is the value to be calculated; but if an overflow occurs, the solution is obtained by adding the value 1 to the result of the sum (regardless of the overflow bit). Let's look at it with an example. Let's add the value 3 to the value −2 in addition to one:

Coding in complement to one has some disadvantages. One of them is that there are two ways to encode the value 0 (with 8 bits, for example, both 00000000 and 11111111 represent the value 0) and, therefore, we can only represent 255 values ([−127, 127]), instead of 256. But the main drawback is the slowness with which operations are carried out as the sum: when there is an overflow, two additions have to be made, that is, twice as much time must be invested.

An alternative coding (and that is the one used in computers) is called ((complement two)). To change the sign to a number we have to invert all its bits and add 1 to the result. This coding, which seems unnatural, has the advantages that there is only one way to represent the null value (the range of values represented is [−128, 127]) and, mainly, that a single operation In sum, it is enough to obtain the correct result of an addition. Repeat the previous example. Add 3 and −2, but in addition to two:

11111

00000011

11111110 (1) 0000000 1

If we ignore the overflowed bit, the result is correct.

Well, we have already talked a lot about how to code numbers (although later we will offer some reflection on how to represent values with a fractional part). Let's worry for a moment about how to represent text. There is a table that maps 127 symbols with bit sequences and has been assumed to be standard. It is the so-called ASCII table, whose name is the acronym for (American Standard Code for Information Interchange). The correspondence between sequences of bits and characters determined by the table is arbitrary but accepted as standard. The letter (a), for example, is encoded with bit sequence 01100001 and the letter (A) is encoded with 01000001. The text can then be encoded as a sequence of bits. Here is the text (Hello) encoded with the ASCII table:

01001000 01101111 01101100 01100001

But, when we see that text on the screen, we don't see a sequence of bits, but the letter ((H)), followed by the letter ((o)) ,. . . What we really see is a graphic, a pixel pattern stored in the computer's memory and displayed on the screen. A bit of value 0 can be shown as white and a bit of value 1 as black. The letter ((H)) that you see on the screen, for example, is the display of this bit pattern:

0 1 0000 1 0

0 1 0000 1 0

0 1 0000 1 0

O 111111 O

O 1 OOOO 1 O

O 1 OOOO 1 O

O 1 OOOO 1 O

In computer memory, there is a bit pattern for each character. When the ASCII code 01001000 is detected, the bit pattern corresponding to the graphic representation of the ((H)) is displayed. Truculent, but effective.

Not only can we represent characters with pixel patterns: all computer graphics are simple pixel patterns arranged as a matrix. As you can see, just zeros and ones are enough to encode the information we handle on a computer: numbers, text, images, etc.

1.3. Programs And Programming Languages

Before stopping to talk about the coding of the information we were commenting that the memory is a large store with numbered drawers, that is, identifiable with numerical values: their respective addresses. A sequence of bits of fixed size is stored in each drawer. The CPU, the ((brain)) of the computer, is capable of executing actions specified by a sequence of instructions. An instruction describes a very simple action, in the style of ((add this to that)), ((multiply the quantities in such and such a memory position)), ((leave the result in such address of memory)), ((make a copy of the data of this address in this other address)), ((find out if the amount stored in a certain address is negative)), etc. The instructions are represented by particular combinations of ones and zeros (binary values) and, therefore, can be stored in memory.

By intelligently combining the instructions in a sequence we can make the CPU execute more complex calculations. A sequence of instructions is a program. If there is an instruction to multiply but none to raise a number to the cube, we can build a program that makes this last calculation from the available instructions. Here, roughly, is a sequence of instructions that calculates the cube from products:

Take the number and multiply it by yourself.

Multiply the result of the last operation by the original number.

The sequences of instructions that the computer can execute are called programs in machine code because the programming language in which they are expressed is called machine code. A programming language is any notation system that allows expressing programs.

The reality is increasingly complex. More modern systems store characters in memory in another way, but talking about it means deviating a lot from what we want to tell.

1.3.1. Machine Code

The machine code encodes the sequences of instructions as sequences of ones and waxes that follow certain rules. Each family of computers has its own repertoire of instructions, that is, its own machine code.

A program that, for example, calculates the average of three numbers stored in memory positions 10, 11 and 12, respectively, and leaves the result in memory position 13, could have the following aspect expressed in an understandable way for us:

Add content from addresses 10 and 11 and leave result in address 13

Add content of addresses 13 and 12 and leave result in direction 13

Divide content of address 13 by 3 and leave result in direction 13

Stop

In reality, the content of each address would be coded as a series of ones and zeros, so the real aspect of a program like the one described above could be this:

10101011 00001010 00001011 00001101

10101011 00001101 00001100 00001101

00001110 00001101 00000011 00001101

00000000 00000000 00000000 00000000

The CPU is an ingenious electronic circuit system capable of interpreting the meaning of each of these bit sequences and carrying out the actions they encode. When the CPU executes the program, it starts with the instruction contained in the first of its memory locations. Once you have executed an instruction, move on to the next one, and continue this way until you find an instruction that stops the execution of the program.

Assume that values 5, 10 and 6 have been stored in memory addresses 10, 11 and 12, respectively. We represent thus the memory:

Add content from addresses 10 and 11 and leave result in address 13

Add content of addresses 13 and 12 and leave result in address 13

Divide content of address 13 by 3 and leave result in address 13

Stop

Naturally, the values of positions 10, 11 and 12 would be coded in binary, although we have chosen to represent them in base 10 for the sake of clarity. Program execution proceeds as follows:

First, the instruction of address 1 is executed, which says that we take the content of address 10 (value 5), add it to that of address 11 (value 10) and leave the result (value 15) in the memory address 13. After executing this first instruction, the memory is thus:

Add content from addresses 10 and 11 and leave result in address 13

Add content of addresses 13 and 12 and leave result in address 13

Divide content of address 13 by 3 and leave result in address 13

Stop

Next, the instruction of address 2 is executed, which orders that the content of address 13 (value 15) be taken, is added to the content of address 12 (value 6) and the result (value 21) is deposited in address 13. The memory becomes in this state.

Add content from addresses 10 and 11 and leave result in address 13

Add content of addresses 13 and 12 and leave result in address 13

Divide content of address 13 by 3 and leave result in address 13

Stop

Now, the third instruction says that we have to take the value of address 13 (value 21), divide it by 3 and deposit the result (value 7) in address 13. This is the state in What is left of the memory after executing the third instruction:

Add content from addresses 10 and 11 and leave result in address 13

Add content of addresses 13 and 12 and leave result in address 13

Divide content of address 13 by 3 and leave result in address 13

Stop

And finally, the CPU stops the execution of the program, because it encounters the Stop instruction at address 4.

1.3.2. Assembly Language

In the early stages of computer science, programs were entered directly into the computer in the computer code, indicating one by one the value of the bits of each of the memory locations. To do this, cables were manually inserted in a connector panel: each cable inserted into a connector represented a one and each connector without a cable represented a zero. As you can imagine, programming a computer like this was an arduous task, extremely tedious and prone to error commissioning. The slightest failure led to an incorrect program. Soon notations were designed that simplified programming: each machine code instruction was represented by a mnemonic code, that is, an abbreviation easily identifiable with the purpose of instruction.

For example, the program developed before could be represented as the following text:

SUM # 10, # 11, # 13
SUM # 13, # 12, # 13
DIV # 13, 3, # 13
FINISH

In this language, the word SUM represents the instruction to add, DIV the one to divide and END represents the instruction that indicates that the execution of the program must end. The pad (#) in front of a number indicates that we want to access the contents of the memory location whose address is said number. The characters that represent the program are entered in the computer memory with the help of a keyboard and each letter is stored in a memory position as a particular combination of ones and zeros (its ASCII code, for example).

But how can this type of program be executed if the sequence of ones and zeros that describes it as the text does not constitute a valid program in machine code? With the help of another program: the assembler. The assembler is a translator program that reads the contents of the memory addresses in which we have stored mnemonic codes and writes in other memory positions its associated instructions in machine code.

The repertoire of mnemonic codes translatable machine code and the rules that allow combining them, expressing addresses, coding numerical values, etc., is called assembly language and is another programming language.

1.3.3. A Different Program for Each Computer?

Unless the CPU has been specifically designed to reproduce the operation of the former, as is the case with AMD processors, designed with the objective of executing the machine code of Intel processors.

For example, adding instructions that facilitate the programming of multimedia applications (as with the Intel Pentium MMX and later models) unthinkable when the first CPU in the family was designed (the Intel 8086).

Hello World!

We would like to show you the appearance of programs written in real assembly languages with a couple of examples. It is a tradition to illustrate the different programming languages with a simple program that merely displays the message ((Hello, World!))

So we'll follow her. Here is that program written in the assembly languages of two different CPUs: on the left, that of the Intel 80x86 processors (whose last representative for the moment is Pentium 4) and on the right, that of the processors of the Motorola 68000 family (which is the processor of the first Apple Macintosh computers).

.data

msg:

.string "Hello, World! \ n"

```
len:
.long. - msg
.text
.globl _start
_start:
push $ len
push $ msg
push $ 1
movl $ 0x4,% eax
call _syscall
addl $ 12,% esp
push $ 0
movl $ 0x1,% eax
call _syscall
_syscall:
int $ 0x80
ret
start:
move.l #msg, - (a7)
move.w # 9, - (a7)
trap # 1
addq.l # 6, a7
move.w # 1, - (a7)
trap # 1
addq.l # 2, a7
```

```
clr - (a7)
trap # 1
msg: dc.b "Hello, World!", 10,13,0
```

As you can see, both programs have a very different aspect. On the other hand, the two are quite long (between 10 and 20 lines) and difficult to understand and translatable to the machine code of any computer. Having this language will allow you to write the programs only once and execute them on different computers after making the corresponding translations to each machine code with different training programs.

If the idea is in principle interesting, it has serious drawbacks:

A universal assembly language cannot take into account how computers will be designed in the future and what type of instructions they will support, so it may become obsolete in a short time.

Programming in assembly language (even in that so-called universal assembly language) is complicated by the many details that must be taken into account.

In addition, put to design a general programming language, why not use a natural language, that is, a language such as Spanish or English? Programming a computer would simply consist of writing (or pronouncing in front of a microphone!) A text in which we indicate what we want the computer to do using the same language with which we communicate with others. A computer program could be responsible for translating our sentences into the machine code, in the same way that an assembly program translates machine code assembly language. It is an attractive idea but that is far from what we know how to do for several reasons:

The intrinsic complexity of the constructions of natural languages greatly hinders the synthetic analysis of sentences, that is, understanding their structure and how the different elements that constitute them are related to each other.

The semantic analysis, that is, the understanding of the meaning of the sentences, is even more complicated. The ambiguities and inaccuracies of natural language make its sentences easily pre-sentence different meanings, even when we can analyze them synthetically. (How many meanings does the phrase ((Work in a bank.))?) Without a good understanding of the meaning, it is not possible to make an acceptable translation.

1.3.4. High Level Programming Languages

There is an intermediate solution: we can design programming languages that, without being as powerful and expressive as natural languages, eliminate much of the complexity of assembly languages and are well adapted to the type of problems that we can solve with computers: the so-called high-level programming languages. The qualifier ((high level)) indicates its independence from a specific computer. By contrast, machine codes and assembly languages are called low-level programming languages.

Here is the program that calculates the average of three numbers in a typical high-level language (Python):

```
a = 5
b = 10
c = 6
mean = (a + b + c) / 3
```

The first three lines define the three values and the fourth calculates the average. As you can see, it is much more readable than a program in machine code or in an assembly language.

For each high-level language and for each CPU a program can be written that translates the instructions of the high-level language into machine code instructions, thereby achieving the desired independence of the programs with respect to the different computer systems. Only one version of the program will have to be written in a high-level programming language and the translation of that program into the machine code of each CPU will be done automatically.

1.3.5. Compilers and Interpreters

We have said that high-level languages are automatically translated in machine code, yes, but you have to know that there are two different types of translators depending on their mode of operation: compilers and interpreters.

A compiler fully reads a program in a high-level language and translates it in its entirety to an equivalent machine code program. The resulting machine code program can be executed as many times as desired, without the need to translate the original program again.

An interpreter acts in a different way: he reads a program written in a high-level language, instruction to instruction and, for each of them, translates to the instructions I hate equivalent machines and execute them immediately. There is no translation process completely separate from the execution process. Each time we execute the program with an interpreter, the translation and execution process is repeated, since both are simultaneous.

Compilers and interpreters. . . of languages

It may be helpful to establish an analogy between compilers and interpreters of programming languages and translators and interpreters of languages.

A compiler acts as a translator who receives a book written in a specific language (high-level language) and writes a new book that, as faithfully as possible, contains a translation of the original text into another language (machine code). The translation (compilation) process takes place only once and we can read the book (run the program) in the target language (machine code) as many times as we want.

A program interpreter acts as your counterpart in the case of languages. Suppose an English conference is given in different cities and an interpreter offers simultaneous translation into Spanish. Each time the conference is delivered, the interpreter must perform the translation again. Moreover, the translation is produced on the fly, sentence by sentence, and not at a stretch at the end of the conference. In the same way, an interpreter of a programming language acts: it translates every time we execute the program and also does instruction to instruction.

As a general rule, the interpreters will execute the programs more slowly, since the one that consumes the simultaneous translation is added to the execution time of the machine code. In addition, a compiler can examine the high-level program covering more than one instruction every time, so it is capable of producing better translations. An interpreted program is usually much slower than another one that has been compiled (typically between 2 and 100 times slower!).

If it is so slow to interpret a program, why are not compilers only used? It is early for you to understand the reasons, but, as a general rule, interpreters allow greater flexibility than compilers and certain high-level programming languages have been designed to exploit that greater flexibility. Other programming languages, on the other hand, sacrifice flexibility for the sake of faster execution. Although nothing prevents us from compiling or interpreting any programming language, certain languages are considered appropriate for the translation to be carried out with a compiler and others not. It is more appropriate to speak, then, of typically interpreted programming languages and typically compiled programming languages. Among the first, we can mention Python, BASIC, Perl, Tcl, Ruby, Bash, Java or Lisp. Between the seconds, C, Pascal, C ++ or Fortran.

In this course we will learn to program using two different programming languages: one interpreted, Python, and another compiled, C. This volume is dedicated to the programming language with Python. Another volume of the same collection is dedicated to the study of C, but on the basis that it is already known to program with Python.

1.3.6. Python

There are many other programming languages, why learn Python? Python has a series of advantages that make it very attractive, both for professional use and for learning programming. Among the most interesting from the educational point of view we have:

Python is a very expressive language, that is, Python programs are very compact: a Python program is usually quite shorter than its equivalent in languages such as C. (Python is considered by many to be a programming language of very high level.)

Python is very readable. Python syntax is very elegant and allows the writing of programs whose reading is easier than if we used other programming languages.

Python offers an interactive environment that facilitates testing and helps clear up doubts about certain language features.

The Python runtime environment tecta many of the programming errors that are in the control of the compilers and provides very rich information to detect and correct them.

Python can be used as a procedural imperative language or as an object-oriented language. It has a rich set of data structures that can be easily manipulated. These features make it relatively easy to translate calculation methods into Python programs.

Python has been designed by Guido van Rossum and is in a process of continuous development by a large developer community. Approximately every six months a new version of Python is published. Quiet! It is not that every half year the programming language is radically changed, but that it is enriched while maintaining compatibility with the programs written for earlier versions. We will use features of Python version 2.3, so you should use that version or higher.

A fundamental advantage of Python is the gratuitousness of its interpreter. You can download the web interpreter page from http://www.python.org . The Python interpreter has versions for virtually any platform in use: PC systems under Linux, PC systems under Microsoft Windows, Apple Macintosh systems, etc.

To get you to the idea of what a complete Python program presents, we present one that calculates the average of three numbers that the user enters by keyboard and shows the result on the screen:

a = float (raw_input ('Give me a number:'))

b = float (raw_input ('Give me another number:')) c = float (raw_input ('And now, one more:'))

mean = (a + b + c) / 3

print 'The average is', average

In recent years Python has experienced a significant increase in the number of programmers and companies that use it. Here are some quotes that have headed for some time the official Python website (http://www.python.org):

Python has been an important part of Google from the beginning, and it continues to be as the system grows and evolves. Today, dozens of Google engineers use Python and we are still looking for skilled people in this language.

Peter Norvig, director of search quality at Google Inc.

Python plays a key role in our production chain. Without him, a project of the scope of ((Star Wars: Episode II)) would have been very difficult to move forward. Crowd visualization, batch process, scene composition. . . Python is what unites everything.

Tommy Brunette, senior technical director of Industrial Light & Magic.

Python is everywhere in Industrial Light & Magic. It is used to extend the capacity of our applications and to provide the tail that joins them. Every computer-generated image we create includes Python at some point in the process.

1.3.7. C

The programming language C is one of the most used in the professional world. Most commercial and free applications have been developed with the programming language C. The Linux operating system, for example, has been developed in C in its entirety.

Why is the C language so used? C is a general-purpose language that allows controlling with great precision the factors that influence the efficiency of the programs. But this control capacity ((fine)) offered by C has a price: writing programs can be much more expensive since we have to be aware of numerous details. So n is so that many programmers claim that C is not a high-level language, but an intermediate level.

Hello again, world!

We present the programs ((Hello, world!)) In Python (left) and C (right).

```
print 'Hello, world!'
#inclu of <stdio.h>
int main (void) {
printf ("Hello, world! \ n");
return 0;
}
```

As you can see, Python seems to go directly to the problem: a single line.

We will start learning Python.

Here you have a C version of the calculation of the average of three numbers read by keyboard:

```
#include <stdio.h>
int main (void)
{
double a, b, c, mean;
printf ("Give me a number:");
scanf ("% lf", & a);
printf ("Give me another number:");
scanf ("% lf", & b);
printf ("And now, one more:");
```

```
scanf ("% lf", & c);
mean = (a + b + c) / 3;
printf ("The average is% f \ n", average);
return 0;
}
```

C has undergone an evolution since its design in the 1970s. The C, as conceived by its authors, Brian Kernighan, and Dennis Ritchie, of the North American telecommunication company AT&T, is popularly known as K&R C and is practically obsolete. In the 1980s, C was modified and standardized by the American National Standards Institute (ANSI), which resulted in the so-called ANSI C and is now known as C89 for the year in which it was published. The standard was revised in the 90s and new features were incorporated that significantly improve the language. The result is the second edition of ANSI C, more known as C99. This is the version we will study in this course.

In the subject, we will use a free C compiler: the gcc in its version 3.2 or higher. Initially, gcc was named as taking the acronym for GNU C Compiler. GNU is the name of a project that aims to offer an operating system ((free)) and all the tools that it is common to find on a Unix platform. Today, the GNU / Linux platform, which is composed of a core operating system of the Unix family (Linux) and numerous tools developed as part of the GNU project, including gcc, has become very popular. The version of gcc that we will use does not support even all the features of C99, but only those that we will learn in the course.

Any recent distribution of Linux 5 incorporates the version of gcc that we will use or higher. You can download a version of gcc and the associated utilities for Microsoft Windows at http://www.delorie.com/djgpp. On page http://www.bloodshed.net/devcpp.html you will find an integrated environment (text editor, code debugger, compiler, etc.) that also uses the gcc compiler.

Be careful, not all compilers support some features of the latest version of C, so you may experience a compatibility problem if you use a different compiler than the one we recommend.

1.4. Beyond The Programs: Algorithms

Two programs that solve the same problem expressed in the same or in different programming languages but that follow, basically, the same procedure, are two implementations of the same algorithm. An algorithm is simply a sequence of steps aimed at achieving an objective.

When designing an algorithm, we can express it in any one of the many general-purpose programming languages that exist. However, this is not very appropriate:

Not all programmers know all languages and there is no consensus on which is the most appropriate to express solutions to different problems, any of the programming languages have particularities that can interfere with a clear and concise expression of the solution to a problem. We can express the algorithms in natural language, because the objective is to communicate a decisive procedure to other people and, eventually, translate them into some language of Babel's tower.

We have said that high-level programming languages intended, among other objectives, to alleviate the problem of each computer using its own machine code. As a result, you may be surprised by the number of programming languages cited. Well, the ones we have quoted are a few of the most used: there are hundreds! Why so many?

The first high-level programming language was Fortran, which was designed in the first 50s (it is still used today, although in evolved versions). Fortran was designed with the purpose of translating machine-related mathematical formulas (in fact, its name comes from FORmula TRANslator, that is, translator of formulas). Soon other programming languages were designed for specific purposes: Cobol (Common Business Oriented Language), Lisp (List Processing language), etc. Each of these languages made it easy to write programs to solve problems in particular areas: Cobol for business management problems, Lisp for certain Artificial Intelligence problems, etc. There were also efforts to design ((general purpose)) languages, that is, applicable to any domain, such as Algol 60 (Algorithmic Language). In the decade of the 60s, new programming languages appeared (Algol 68, Pascal, Simula 67, Snobol 4, etc.), but perhaps the most notable of this decade was that the theoretical bases of the compiler and interpreter design were laid. When the technology for the design of these tools became accessible to more and more programmers, there was an authentic staging in the number of programming languages. Already in 1969, about 120 programming languages had been designed and compilers or interpreters had been implemented for each of them.

The existence of so many programming languages created a situation similar to that of the tower of Babel: each laboratory or computer department used a programming language and there was no way to exchange programs.

Over the years, a selection of those most appropriate programming languages has been produced for each type of task and many others have been designed that synthesize what has been learned from previous languages. The most used today are C, C ++, Java, Python, Perl, and PHP.

If you are curious, you can see examples of the program ((Hello, world!)) In more than one center of different programming languages (and more than four hundred dialects) by visiting page http: // www.uni-karlsruhe.de/ ~ uu9r / lang / html / lang-all.en.html

If, for example, we want to calculate the average of three keypad numbers we can follow this algorithm:

request the value of the first number,

request the value of the second number,

request the value of the third number,

add the three numbers and divide the result by 3,

Show the result.

As you can see, this sequence of operations defines exactly the process that allows us to perform the proposed calculation and that we have already implemented as programs in Python and C. The algorithms are independent of the programming language. They describe a procedure that you can implement in any general-purpose programming language or, even, that you can execute by hand with pencil, paper and, perhaps, the help of a calculator.

It is not true that any procedure described step by step can be considered an algorithm. An algorithm must satisfy certain conditions. An analogy with recipes (procedures for preparing dishes) will help you understand these restrictions. Study this first recipe:

put oil in a pan,

Light the fire,

heat the oil,

catch an egg

break the shell,

pour the contents of the egg into the pan,

season with salt,

Wait for it to look good.

In principle, it is already: with the recipe, its ingredients and the necessary tools we are able to cook a dish. Well, not quite true, as there are a few issues that are not entirely clear in our recipe:

What type of egg do we use? A chicken egg? A frog egg?

How much salt do we use ?: a pinch? a kilo?

How much oil should we pour into the pan ?: a cubic centimeter? a liter?

What is the result of the process? Does the pan with the cooked egg and the oil?

In a recipe, we have to make clear what ingredients we have and what the final result is. In an algorithm, we must specify what the problem data (input data) and what result we are going to produce (output data).

This new recipe corrects those bugs:

Ingredients: 10 cc. of olive oil, a chicken and a pinch of salt.

Method:

wait for the chicken to lay an egg,

put oil in a pan,

Light the fire,

heat the oil,

catch the egg,

break the shell,

pour the contents of the egg into the pan,

season with salt,

Wait for it to look good.

Presentation: deposit the fried egg, without oil, on a plate.

But the recipe is still not quite right. There are certain uncertainties in the recipe:

How hot should the oil be at the time of pouring the egg, smoking, burning?

How long to wait? a second? until the egg is blackened?

And even worse, are we sure that the chicken will lay an egg? It could happen that the chicken did not lay any eggs.

In order for the recipe to be complete, we should specify with absolute precision each of the steps that lead to the achievement of the objective and, in addition, each of them should be achievable in finite time.

It is not enough to say more or less how to achieve the objective: it is necessary to say exactly how each step must be executed and, in addition, each step must be realizable in a finite time. This new recipe corrects some of the problems of the previous one, but presents others of different nature:

Ingredients: 10 cc. of olive oil, a chicken egg and a pinch of salt.

Method:

put oil in a pan,

light the fire at medium gas,

heat the oil until it smokes slightly,

catch an egg

break the shell with the power of the mind, without touching the egg,

pour the contents of the egg into the pan,

season with salt,

Wait for it to look good.

Presentation: deposit the fried egg, without oil, on a plate.

The fifth step is not feasible. To break an egg you have to use something more than ((the power of the mind)). In every algorithm, you must use only instructions that can be carried out.

Here is a recipe in which all the steps are realizable:

Ingredients: 10 cc. of olive oil, a chicken egg and a pinch of salt.

Method:

put oil in a pan,

tune to a music station on the radio,

light the fire am gas,

take a solo game,

heat the oil until it smokes slightly,

catch an egg

break the shell,

pour the contents of the egg into the pan,

season with salt,

Wait for it to look good.

Presentation: deposit the fried egg, without oil, on a plate.

In this new recipe, there are actions that, although expressed with sufficient precision and being realizable, do nothing useful to reach our goal (tune the radio and play cards). In an algorithm, each step taken should lead and bring us closer to achieving the objective.

There is an additional consideration that we have to do, although in principle it seems obvious: every well-constructed algorithm must end after the execution of a finite number of steps.

Although all the steps are of finite duration, a sequence of instructions may require infinite time. Think of this method to become a millionaire:

buy a valid lottery number for the next draw,

wait for the draw day,

collate the winning number with ours,

if they are different, return to step 1; Otherwise, we are millionaires.

As you can see, each step of the method requires a finite amount of time, but there is no guarantee of achieving the proposed objective.

From now on, we will no longer be interested in cooking recipes or procedures to enrich themselves effortlessly (at least not as an object of study of the subject!). The algorithms in which we will be interested are those that describe executable calculation procedures on a computer. This will limit the scope of our study to the manipulation and calculation of data (numerical, text, etc.).

An algorithm must have the following characteristics:

Abu Ja'far Mohammed ibn Mˆusˆa Al-Khowˆarizm and Euclid

The word algorithm originates in the name of a 9th-century Persian mathematical mathematician: Abu Ja'far Mohammed ibn Mˆusˆa Al-Khowˆarizm (meaning ((Mohammed, father of Ja'far, son of Moses, born in Khowˆarizm))). Al-Khowˆarizm wrote treatises on arithmetic and ´algebra. Thanks to Al-Khowˆarizm's texts, the Hindus numbering system was introduced in the Arab world and, later, in the West.

In the thirteenth century, the books Carmen de Algorismo (a treatise on arithmetic in verse!) And Algorismus Vulgaris were published, based in part on the Arithmetic of Al-Khowˆarizm. Al-Khowˆarizm also wrote the book ((Kitab al jabr w'al-muqabala)) (((Restoration and reduction rules))), which gave rise to a word you already know: algebra.

Abelardo de Bath, one of the first translators of Latin Al-Khowˆarizm, began a text with ((Dixit Algorismi...)) (((Said Algorism...))), Popularizing thus the term al-gorismo which happened to mean ((making calculations with numerals hindo-ar´abigos)). In the middle ages the abaquistas calculated with ´abaco and the algorithmists with algorithms.

In any case, the concept of algorithm is much earlier than Al-Khow^arizm. In the century 5888 B.C., Euclid proposed in his treatise ((Elements)) a systematic method for the calculation of the Greatest Common Divider (GCF) of two numbers. The method, as proposed by Euclid, says: ((Given two natural numbers, a and b, check if both are equal. If so, a is the GCF. If not, if a is greater than b, subtract aa from the value of b; but if a is less than b, subtract ab from the value of a. Repeat the process with the new values of a and b)). This method is known as ((Euclid's algorithm)), although it is common to find, under that same name, an alternative and more efficient procedure: ((Given two natural numbers, a and b, check if b is zero. If so, a is the GCF. If not, calculate c, the remainder divide by b. Replace a by b by c and repeat the process)).

It must have zero or more input data.

You must provide one or more output data as a result.

Each step of the algorithm must be precisely defined, without the slightest ambiguity.

It must be finite, that is, it must end after the execution of a finite number of steps, each of which must be executable in finite time.

It must be effective, that is, each of its steps must be able to be executed in finite time with certain resources (in our case, with those provided by a computer system).

In addition, we are interested in the algorithms being efficient, that is, that they reach their objective or as quickly as possible and with the least consumption of resources.

Chapter 2
An Advanced Calculator

"Do you know how to add?" " Asked the White Queen." How much is one plus one plus one plus one plus one plus one plus one plus one plus one plus one plus one plus one as one plus one? "I don't know", Alicia said. I lost count.

"He doesn't know how to make an addition," the Red Queen interrupted.

- Lewis Carroll, Alice through the mirror.

The objective of this topic is that you familiarize yourself with the interactive Python environment, that you learn to build arithmetic expressions by storing the results in variables through assignments and that you know the basic data types of the Python programming language.

2.1. Interactive Sessions

When we program, we use a set of tools that we call the programming environment. Among these tools we have text editors (which allow us to write programs), compilers or interpreters (which translate the machine code programs), debuggers (which help detect errors), runtime analyzers (to study the efficiency of the programs), etc.

Interpreted languages often offer an interactive execution tool. With it, it is possible to give orders directly to the interpreter and obtain an immediate response for each of them. That is, it is not necessary to write a complete program to start obtaining execution results, but we can ((dialogue)) with the interpreter of our programming language: we ask you to execute an order and respond to us With its result. The interactive environment is a great help to experiment with program fragments before including them in a definitive version. In this section, we will see how to conduct interactive work sessions with Python.

If we have installed Python on our computer, we can start a work session by typing python in the Unix command line. 2 The system will respond by giving us an informative message about the Python version that we are using (and when it was compiled, with what compiler, etc.) and then will show the prompt :

$ python

Type "help", "copyright", "credits" or "license" for more information.

The prompt is the series of characters ((>>>)) that appears in the last line. The prompt indicates that the Python interpreter expects us to enter an order using the keyboard. Abusing language, we will call Python interchangeably to the programming environment, the language interpreter and the programming language itself.

In the Microsoft Windows environment, you can start the interactive interpreter by activating the corresponding icon (which is a cartoon of a python snake) or by selecting the program from the menu ((Start)).

The Unix Python Order

We have invoked the interactive environment by typing python in the Unix command line and pressing the carriage return. When you do this, the Unix command execution environment (often referred to as shell) searches the computer for an application called python and executes it. This application is a program that reads a line entered by keyboard, interprets it as if it were a Python program fragment and displays the result obtained on the screen. (Actually it does more. We will see them already).

As a general rule, the python application resides in / u sr / local / bin / or in / usr / bin /. They are directories where the shell normally looks for programs. If, when writing python and giving the carriage return, the interpreter does not start, make sure the Python environment is installed. If so, you can try to run the environment by giving the full path to the program: for example / usr / local / bin / python.

Let's write an arithmetic expression, for example ((2 + 2)), and press the carriage return key. When we show interactive sessions we will highlight the text that the user types with text on a gray background, we will represent with the symbol (()) the press of the carriage return key. Python evaluates the expression (that is, gets its result) and responds by displaying the result on the screen.

>>>

```
2 + 2

4

>>>
```

The last line is, again, the prompt: Python just executed the last order (evaluate an expression and show the result) and asks us to enter a new order.

If we want to end the interactive session and exit the Python interpreter, we must enter an end of file mark, which in Unix is indicated by pressing the control key and, without releasing it, also the d key. (From now on we will represent a combination of keys like the one described thus: Cd.)

End of file

The ((end of file mark)) indicates that a file has finished. But we don't work with a file, but with the keyboard! Actually, the computer considers the keyboard as a file. When we want ((close the keyboard)) for an application, we send an end of file mark from the keyboard. On Unix, the end of file mark is sent by pressing Cd; in MS-DOS or Microsoft Windows, pressing Cz.

There is another way to end the session; writes from sys import exit ()

In English, ((exit)) means ((exit)). Yes, but what does ((from sys import exit)) mean and why is there a couple of parentheses of the word ((exit)) in the second line? Later we will find out.

2.1.1. Arithmetic Operators

The addition and subtraction operations, for example, are denoted by the symbols or operators + and -, respectively and operate on two numerical values (the operands). Let's try some expressions formed with these two operators:

>>>

1 + 2

3

1 + 2 + 3

6

1-2 + 3

2

Note that you can enter several operations on the same line or expression. The order in which the operations are carried out is (in principle) from left to right. The expression 1 - 2 + 3, for example, is mathematically equivalent to ((1 - 2) + 3); That is why we say that addition and subtraction are associative operators on the left.

We can graphically represent the order of application of operations using synthetic trees. A synthetic tree is a graphic representation in which we have operators and operands as nodes and in which each operator is connected to its operands. The synthetic tree of the expression ((1 - 2 + 3)) is this.

The top node of a tree is called the root node. Nodes labeled with operators (represented by circles) are called interior nodes. The inner nodes have one or more child or descendant nodes (of which they are their respective parent or ascendant nodes). These nodes are root nodes of other (sub) synthetic trees (the definition of a synthetic tree is self-referential!). The values resulting from evaluating the expressions associated with said (sub) trees constitute the operands of the operation that represent the inner node. Nodes without descendants are called terminal nodes or leaves (represented by squares) and correspond to numerical values.

The evaluation of each individual operation in the synthetic tree ((flows)) of the leaves towards the root (the upper node); that is, in the first place the subexpression ((1 - 2)) is evaluated, which corresponds to the deepest subtree. The result of the evaluation is −1.

Next, the subexpression that adds the result of evaluating ((1 - 2)) to the value 3 is evaluated:

+

−1 - 3

1 + 2

Thus the final result is obtained: the value 2.

If we want to calculate (1 - (2 + 3)) we can do so by adding parentheses to the arithmetic expression:

1- (2 + 3)

-4

The synthetic tree of this new expression is

-

1 + 2 + 3

In this new tree, the first underexpression evaluated is that corresponding to the right subtree. Note that the expression brackets do not appear in the synthetic tree. The synthetic tree already indicates the order in which the different operations are processed and does not need parentheses. The Python expression, however, needs the brackets to indicate that same order of evaluation.

The addition and subtraction operators are binary, that is, they operate on two operands. The same symbol that is used for subtraction is also used for a unary operator, that is, an operator acting on a single operand: the sign change, which returns the value of its changed operand of sign. Here are some examples:

>>> -3

-3

>>> - (1 -3)

>>> 2

Note that these operators are also associative on the left: the expression ((3 * 4/2)).

If operators follow precedence rules that determine their order of application, what do we do when we want a different order of application? Use parentheses, as we do with conventional mathematical notation.

2.1.2. Click errors and exceptions

When we introduce an expression and give the order to evaluate it, we may be mistaken. If we have incorrectly formed an expression, Python will indicate it to us with an error message. The error message provides information about the type of error committed and the place where it has been detected. Here you have an erroneous expression and the corresponding error message:

(1 + 2)

File "<stdin>", line 1

(1 + 2)

^

SyntaxError: invalid syntax

In this example, we have closed a parenthesis when there was no other one previously opened, which is incorrect. Python tells us that it has detected a syntax error (SyntaxError) and ((points)) with an arrow (the character r) to the place where it is located. (The text ((File "<stdin>", line 1)) indicates that the error occurred when reading from the keyboard, that is, the standard input —stdin is an abbreviation for English ((standard input)), which is translated by ((standard entry)) -.)

In Python, errors are called exceptions. When Python is unable to analyze an expression, it produces an exception. When the interactive interpreter detects the exception, it displays an error message on the screen.

Let's look at some other errors and the messages produced by Python.

```
1 + * 3
File "<stdin>", line 1
1 + * 3
     ^
SyntaxError: invalid syntax
>>>
2 + 3%
File "<stdin>", line 1
2 + 3%
     ^
SyntaxError: invalid syntax
>>>
1 / 0
Traceback (innermost last):
File "<stdin>", line 1, in?
ZeroDivisionError: integer division or module
```

In the example, the last error is of a different nature from the previous ones (there is no character pointing to any place): it is a zero division error (ZeroDivisionError) when the others were

Synthetic errors (SyntaxError). The amount that results from dividing by zero is not defined and Python is unable to calculate value as a result of the 1/0 expression. It is not a synthetic error because the expression is synthetically well-formed: the division operator has two operands, as he plays.

Advanced edition in the interactive environment

When we are writing an expression we may make mistakes and detect them before requesting their evaluation. We will still be in time to correct them. The delete key, for example, removes the character to the left of the cursor. You can move the cursor to any point on the line you are editing using the cursor movement keys left and right. The text you type will always be inserted just to the left of the cursor.

So far we have had to type each evaluated expression from scratch, even though many were quite similar to each other. We can type less if we learn to use some advanced editing functions.

The first thing we need to know is that the Python interactive interpreter memorizes each of the expressions evaluated in an interactive session in case we want to retrieve them later. The list of expressions we have evaluated constitutes the history of the interactive session. You can ((navigate)) through the story using the cursor up and down arrow keys. Each time you press the scroll up key you will recover an older expression. The scroll down key allows you to retrieve more recent expressions. The recovered expression will appear at the prompt and you could modify it as you wish.

2.2 Data Types

We are going to carry out a curious result experiment:

3/2

1

The result of dividing 3 by 2 should not be 1, without or 1.5! What has happened? Was Python wrong? No. Python has acted following precise rules in which a new concept participates: the type of data.

2.2.1. Whole And Floating

Each value used by Python is of a certain type. So far we have only used integer data, that is, without decimals. When an operation is carried out, Python takes into account the type of the operands when producing the result. If the two operands are of the integer type, the result is also of the integer type, so the integer division between the integers 3 and 2 produces the integer value 1.

If we want to obtain real-type results, we must use real operands. Real operands must, in principle, have a decimal part, even if this is null.

3.0 / 2.0

1.5

There are differences between integers and reals in Python beyond that the former do not have decimals and the latter does. Number 3 and number 3.0, for example, are indistinguishable in mathematics, but they are different in Python. What differences are there?

The integers usually occupy less memory.

Transactions between integers are generally faster.

So, we will use integers unless we really need numbers with decimals. We have to specify something about the denomination of numbers with decimals: the term ((real)) is not adequate since it leads to thinking about the real numbers of mathematics. In mathematics, real numbers can present infinite decimals, and that is impossible on a computer. When working with computers we will have to settle for mere approximations to the real numbers.

Remember that everything on the computer is sequences of zeros and ones. We must, therefore, internally represent with them the approximations to the real numbers. To facilitate data exchange, all conventional computers use the same coding, that is, they represent the approximations to real numbers in the same way. This encoding is known as ((IEEE Standard 754 floating point)) (which can be translated by ((Standard IEEE 754 for floating-point))), so we will call numbers in floating-point format or Simply floating to numbers with decimals that we can represent with the computer.

A floating number must be specified following certain rules. In principle, it consists of two parts: mantissa and exponent. The exponent is separated from the mantissa with the letter ((e)) (or ((E))). For example, the floating number 2e3 (or 2E3) has mantissa 2 and exponent 3 and represents the number $2 \cdot 10^3$, that is, 2000.

The exponent can be negative: 3.2e-3 is $3.2 \cdot 10$ −3, that is, 0.0032. Keep in mind that if a floating number has no exponent, it must have a fractional part. Ah! A couple of rules: if the whole part of the number is null, the float can start directly with a point, and if the fractional part is null, it can end with a point. Let's look at a couple of examples: the number 0.1 can also be written as .1; on the other hand, the number 2.0 can be written as 2., that is, in both cases the zero is optional. Too many rules? Don't worry, with the practice you will end up remembering them.

It is possible to mix data of different types in the same expression.

A warning about typographical agreements. In Spanish, the fractional part of a number is separated from the whole part by a comma, and not by a period. However, the Anglo-Saxon standard indicates that the point should be used. Python follows this rule, so the number in Spanish denoted as 1.5 must be written as 1.5 for Python to interpret it correctly. In order to avoid confusion, we will always use the point as a character of separation between the whole and fractional part of a number.

IEEE Standard 754

A floating-point number has three components: the sign, the mantissa, and the exponent.

Here is a floating-point number: $-14.1 \times 10 -3$. The sign is negative, the mantissa is 14.1 and the exponent is -3. Normalized floating-point numbers have a mantissa less than or equal to 10. The same number as before, in normalized floating-point, is $-1.41 \times 10 -2$. A usual notation for floating-point numbers replaces the product ($\times$) and the exponent base with the letter ((e)) or ((E)). We will note with -1.41e-2 the number of the example.

Python floats follow the IEEE Standard 754. It is a binary and standardized coding of floating-point numbers and, therefore, with base 2 for the exponent and mantissa of value less than 2. Use 32 bits (simple precision) or 64 bits (double precision) to encode each number. Python uses the double-precision format. In the double-precision format, 1 bit is reserved for the sign of the number, 11 for the exponent and 52 for the mantissa. With this format, numbers as close to zero as $10 -323$ (322 zeros after the decimal point and one) or absolute value as large as 10^308 can be represented.

Not all numbers have an exact representation in the floating-point format.

Observe what happens in this case:

0.1

0.10000000000000001

The maltisa, which is worth 1/10, cannot be represented exactly. In binary we obtain the periodic sequence of bits

0.000110011001100110011001100110011001100110011001100110011. . .

There is, therefore, no way to represent 1/10 with the 52 bits of the double-precision format. In base 10, the first 52 bits of the sequence gives us the value

0.1000000000000000055511151231257827021181583404541015625.

It is as close to 1/10 as we can be. On the screen, Python only shows us its first 17 decimal places (with the corresponding rounding).

An additional peculiarity of the numbers coded with the IEEE 754 standard is that their accuracy is different according to the number represented: the closer to zero, the greater the accuracy. For very large numbers, such precision is lost that there are no decimals (no units, no tens...!). For example, the result of the sum 100000000.0 + 0.000000001 is 100000000.0, and not 100000000.000000001, as you might expect.

In conclusion, you should know that when working with floating numbers it is possible that small errors occur in the representation of the values and during the calculations. This will probably surprise you because it is vox populi que ((computers are never wrong)).

3.0 / 2

1.5

Python follows a simple rule: if there is data of different types, the result is of the type ((more general)). Floats are of type ((more general)) than integers.

1 + 2 + 3 + 4 + 5 + 6 + 0.5

21.5

1 + 2 + 3 + 4 + 5 + 6 + 0.0

21.0

But, attention! It may seem that the rule is not observed in this example:

1.0 + 3/2

2.0

The result should have been 2.5, not 2.0. What happened? Python evaluates the expression step by step. Let us analyze the synthetic tree of that expression:

2.3 Logical And Comparison Operators

floating 2.0

1.0 /

integer 1

The division is a priority over the sum, so this is carried out in the first place. The division has two operands, both of an integer type so it produces an integer result: the value 1. The sum thus receives a floating operand (the one on its left) of value 1.0, and another integer (the result of the division), of value 1. The result is a float and its value is 2.0. What would happen if we ran 1 + 3 / 2.0?

1 + 3 / 2.0

2.5

The synthetic tree is, in this case, floating 2.5

1

3 / 2.0

floating 1.5

Thus, the division provides a floating result, 1.5, which, when added to the integer 1 on the left, provides a new float: 2.5.

Since version 2.3, Python offers a special type of data that allows expressing only two values: true and false. The true value is expressed with True and the false value with False. They are logical or Boolean values. This last name derives from the name of a mathematician, Boole, who developed an algebraic system based on these two values and three operations: conjunction, disjunction, and denial. Python offers support for these operations with logical operators.

There are three logical operators in Python: the ((logical)) or conjunction (and), the ((logical)) or disunion (or) and the ((non-logical))) or denial (not). The and operator results in the true value if and only if its two operands are true.

In the same way that we have used synthetic trees to understand the calculation process of arithmetic operators on integer and floating values, we can use them to interpret the order of evaluation of logical expressions.

There is a family of operators that return Boolean values. Among them, we have the comparison operators, which we study in this section. One of them is the equality operator, which returns True if the compared values are equal. The equality operator is denoted with two consecutive equals: ==. Let's see it running:

```
>>>
2 == 3
False
>>>
2 == 2
True
>>>
```

2.1 == 2.1

True

True == True

True

True == False

False

>>>

2 == 1 + 1

True

Observe the last expression evaluated: it is possible to combine comparison operators and arithmetic operators. Not only that, we can also combine in the same expression logical, arithmetic and comparison operators:

>>> (True or (2 == 1 + 2)) == True True

This is the synthetic tree corresponding to that expression:

== Boolean True

or Boolean True True

True == Boolean False

2 + integer 3

1 + 2

We have indicated next to each inner node the type of the result that corresponds to its subtree.

As you can see, we operate with compatible types at all times.

Before presenting the rules of associativity and precedence that are applicable when combining different types of operators, we present all the comparison operators in Table 2.3 and show you some examples of use:

2 <1

False

1 <2

There is an alternative way to notice the comparison ((it is different from)): you can also use the <> symbol. The comparison of inequality in the programming language C is denoted with! = And in Pascal with <>. Python allows you to use any of the two symbols. In this text we will only use the first.

Comparison operator

Its the same as

! = is different from

< is less than

<= is less than or equal to

> is greater than

> = is greater than or equal to

True

>>>

5 > 1

True

>>>

5 > = 1

True

>>>

5 > 5

False

>>>

5 > = 5

True

>>>

1

! = 0

True

>>>

1

! = 1

False

>>> -2 <= 2

True

It is time for us to present a complete table (table 2.4) with all the operators we know to compare the precedence of each one of them when it appears combined with others.

2.4 Variables And Assignments

Variables and assignments were associative on the left. What would this mean? The sum operator, for example, is associative on the left. When evaluating the arithmetic expression 2 + 3 + 4, proceed as follows: first, add 2 to 3; then, the resulting 5 is added to 4, resulting in a total of 9. If the operator <were associative on the left, the logical expression 2 <3 <4 would be evaluated as follows: first, 2 is compared with 3, resulting in the True value; Then, the result obtained is compared with 4, but what does the expression True <4 mean? Has no sense.

When a sequence of comparators appears, such as 2 <3 <4, Python evaluates it as (2 <3) and (3 <4). This solution allows us to express complex conditions in a simple way and, in cases like the one in this example, it is read in the same way that it would be read with the usual mathematical notation, which seems desirable. But beware! Python allows expressions that are strangers; for example, 2 <3> 1, or 2 <3 == 5.

A rarity of Python: the associativity of comparators

Some common programming languages of use, such as C and C ++, make their comparison operators are associative, so have the problem that expressions such as 0 <1 <4 produce a result that seems illogical. When the comparison operator < is associative on the left, the underexpression 2 <1 is evaluated first. The result is false, which in C and C ++ is represented with the value 0. Then it is evaluated The comparison 0 <4, whose result is. . . true! Thus, for C and C ++ it is true that 2 <1 <4.

Pascal is even more rigid and prohibits expressions such as 2 <1 <4. In Pascal, there is a type of data called boolean whose valid values are true and false. Pascal does not allow to operate between values of different types, so the expression 2 <1 is evaluated at the Boolean value false, which cannot be compared with an integer when trying to calculate the value of false <4. Consequently, an error of types occurs if we try to chain comparisons.

Most of the conventional programming languages choose the C solution or the Pascal solution. When you learn another programming language, it will cost ((undo) you) the elegance with which Python solves the chains of comparisons.

Sometimes we want the computer to remember certain values to use later. For example, suppose we want to perform the calculation of the perimeter and the area of a circle of radius 1.298373 m. The formula of the perimeter is $2\pi r$, where r is the radius, and the formula of the area is πr^2. (We will approximate the value of π with 3.14159265359.) We can perform both calculations as follows:

```
>>> 2 * 3.14159265359
* 1,298373
8.1579181568392176
3.14159265359 * 1.298373 ** 2
```

5.2960103355249037

Note that we have had to enter the values of π and r twice so that, having so many decimals, it is very easy to make mistakes. To alleviate this problem we can use variables:

pi = 3.14159265359

r = 1,298373

>>> 2 * pi * r

8.1579181568392176

>>> pi * r ** 2

5.2960103355249037

In the first line, we have created a variable of name pi and value 3.14159265359. Next, we have created another variable, r, and we have given it the value 1,298373. The act of giving value to a variable is called assignment. By assigning a value to a variable that did not exist, Python reserves a space in memory, stores the value in it and creates an association between the name of the variable and the memory address of that space. We can graphically represent the result of these actions as follows:

pi

3.14159265359

r

1,298373

From that moment, writing pi is equivalent to writing 3.14159265359, and writing r is equivalent to writing 1,298373.

We can store the result of calculating the perimeter and area in variable paths:

pi = 3.14159265359

r = 1,298373

perimeter = 2 * pi * r

area = pi * r ** 2

pi

3.14159265359

r

1,298373

perimeter   8.15791815683921176

area   5.29601033355249037

The memory has been reserved correctly, the corresponding value has been stored in it and the association between the memory and the name of the variable has been established, but we do not get any response on the screen. You should keep in mind that the assignments are ((mute)), that is, they do not cause screen output. If we want to see how much a variable is worth, we can evaluate a former pressure that only contains that variable:

area

5.29601033355249037

Thus, to assign value to a variable, just execute a statement like this:

Variable = expression

Be careful: order is important. Making ((expression = variable)) is not equivalent. An assignment is not a mathematical equation, but an action consisting of (in this order):

evaluate the expression to the right of the equal symbol (=), and save the resulting value in the variable indicated to the left of the equal symbol.

You can assign value to the same variable as many times as you want. The effect is that the variable, at each moment, only ((remember)) the last assigned value. . . until another one is assigned.

a = 1

2 * a

2

is not = (compare is not assign)

When learning to program, many people confuse the assignment operator, =, with the comparison operator, ==. The first is used exclusively to assign a value to a variable. The second, to compare values.

Notice the different response you get by using = y == in the interactive environment:

>>>

a = 10

>>>

to

10

```
>>>
a == 1
False
>>>
to
10
>>>
a + 2
3
>>>
a = 2
>>>
a * a
4
```

An assignment is not an equation

We must insist that the assignments are not mathematical equations, no matter how much they remind us of these. Look at this example, which usually surprises those who start programming:

The first line assigns the variable x the value 3. The second line seems more complicated. If you interpret it as an equation, it makes no sense, because it absurdly concludes that 3 = 4 or, subtracting the x to both sides of the equals, that 0 = 1. But if we follow step by step the actions that Python executes when making an assignment, the thing changes:

The right part of the equal is evaluated (without taking into account the left part at all). The value of x is 3, which added to 1 gives 4.

The result (the 4), is stored in the variable that appears on the left side of the match, that is, in x.

Thus, the result of executing the first two lines is that x is worth 4.

The name of a variable is its identifier. There are precise rules for building identifiers. If they are not followed, we will say that the identifier is not valid. An identifier must consist of 5 lowercase letters , capital letters, digits and / or the underscore (_), with a restriction: that the first character is not a d´ digit.

There is one more rule: an identifier cannot match a reserved word or keyword. A reserved word is a word that has a predefined meaning and is necessary to express certain language constructs. Here is a list of all Python reserved words: and , assert, break, class, continue, def, del, elif, else, except, exec, finally, for, from, global, if, import, in, is, lambda, not, or, pass, print, raise, return, try, while and yield.

For example, the following identifiers are valid: h, x, Z, velocity, acceleration, x, force1, mass_2, _a, a_, test_ 123, typical deviation. You must keep in mind that Python has commands except for symbols that are not typical of the English alphabet, such as accented vowels, the letter '~n', the letter ' c', etc.

It distinguishes between uppercase and lowercase letters, so area, area and AREA are three valid and different identifiers.

Any character other than a letter, a digit or the underscore is invalid in an identifier, including the blank space. For example, the average age (with a space in the middle) is two identifiers (age and average), not one. When an identifier is formed with two words, it is the custom of many programmers to use the underline to separate them: middle_age; Other programmers use a capital letter for the initial of the second: Middle Age. Choose the style you like best to name variables, but stay true to the one you choose.

Since you are free to call a variable with the identifier you want, do it with class: always choose names that are related to the problem data. If, for example, you are going to use a variable to store a distance, call the distance variable and avoid names that mean nothing; in this way, the programs will be more readable.

2.4.1. Assignments with operator

Look at the sentence i = i + 1: apply a unit increase to the content of the variable i. Increasing the value of a variable by any amount is so frequent that there is a compact form in Python. The increase in i can be denoted as follows:

>>> i + = 1

(There can be no space between the + and the =.) You can increase a variable with any quantity, even with one resulting from evaluating an expression.

All arithmetic operators have their assignment with an associated operator.

$z += 2$

$z *= 2$

$z /= 2$

$z -= 2$

$z\% = 2$

$z **= 2$

We must tell you that these compact forms bring nothing new. . . except comfort, so don't worry about having to learn so many things. If you're going to feel uncomfortable having to make decisions and you're always thinking ((do I use the normal or compact form now?)), You better ignore the compact forms at the moment.

More operators!

We have only presented to you the operators that we will use in the text and that you are already prepared to handle. But you must know that there are more operators. There are operators, for example, that are aimed at handling the bit sequences that encode integer values. The binary operator & calculates the operation ((y)) bit by bit, the binary operator | calculates the operation ((or)) bit by bit, the binary operator ^ calculates the ((or exclusive)) (which returns true if and only if the two operands are different), also bit by bit, and the unary operator ~ inverts the bits of its operand. You also have the binary operators << and >>, which shift the bits left or right as many positions as you indicate. These examples will help you understand these operators:

And these operators also present a compact form with assignment: << =, | =, etc.! Later we will study, in addition, the operators is (and is not) and in (and not in), the indexing, call-to-function, cutting operators.

2.4.2. Variables Not Initialized

In Python, the first operation on a variable must be the assignment of a value. You cannot use a variable that has not previously been assigned a value:

a + 2

Traceback (most recent call last):

File "<stdin>", line 1, in?

NameError: name 'a' is not defined

As you can see, an exception NameError is generated, that is, from ((name error)). The explanatory text specifies even more what happened: ((name 'a' is not defined)), that is, ((the name a is not defined)).

The assignment of an initial value to a variable is called initialization of the variable.

We say, then, that in Python it is not possible to use uninitialized variables.

2.5 The Data Type String

So far we have seen that Python can manipulate numerical data of two types: integers and floats. But Python can also manipulate other types of data. We are going to study now the type of data called string. A string is a sequence of characters (letters, numbers, spaces, punctuation marks, etc.) and in Python it is distinguished because it is enclosed in single or double quotes. For example, 'string', 'another example', "1, 2 10 3", '! Yes!', "... Python" are strings. Note that the blanks are shown like this in this text: (()). We do it to make it easy to count the blanks when there are more than one in a row. This chain, for example, consists of three blank spaces: ''.

The chains can be used to represent textual information: names of people, names of colors, car plates ... The chains can also be stored in variables.

name = 'Pepe'

Name

'Pepe'

name 'Pepe'

It is possible to carry out operations with chains. For example, we can ((add)) strings by adding each other.

>>>

'a' + 'b'

'ab'

```
>>>
Name = 'Pepe'
>>>
Name + 'Cano'
'PepeCano'
>>>
Name + " + 'Cano'
'Pepe Cano'
>>>
last name = 'Cano'
>>>
Name + " + last name
'Pepe Cano'
```

Speaking with property, this operation is not called summation, but concatenation . The symbol used is +, the same one we use when adding integers and / or floats; but even if the symbol is the same, keep in mind that adding numbers is not the same as concatenating strings:

```
'12' + '12' '1212'
12 + 12
24
```

Adding or concatenating a string and a numerical value (integer or floating) produces an error:

```
>>> '12' + 12
Traceback (innermost last):
```

File "<stdin>", line 1, in?

TypeError: illegal argument type for built-in operation

And finally, there is a chain repetition operator. The symbol denoting it is *, the same that we have used to multiply integers and/or floats. The repetition operator needs two data: one of type string and one of integer type. The result is the concatenation of the chain I get my sma as many times as the whole number indicates.

A string is not an identifier. With the strings we have a problem: many people who are learning to program confuse a string with a variable identifier and vice versa. They are not the same thing.

Firstly, we assign the variable to the value 1. As a is the name of a variable, that is, an identifier, it is not enclosed in quotes. Then we have written 'a' and Python has also responded with 'a': the a in quotes is a string formed by a single character, the letter ((a)), and has nothing to see with the variable a. Then we have written the letter ((a)) without quotes and Python has responded with the value 1, which is what contains the variable a.

Many programming students make mistakes like these:

They want to use a string, but they forget the quotes, so Python thinks they want to use an identifier; If that identifier does not exist, it gives an error:

Pepe

Traceback (most recent call last):

File "<stdin>", line 1, in?

NameError: name 'Pepe' is not defined

They want to use an identifier but, when in doubt, they enclose it in quotes:

>>> 'x' = 2

SyntaxError: can't assign to literal

Remember: you can only assign values to variables, never to strings, and strings are not identifiers.

>>>

'Hi 5

'Hello Hello hello HELLO HELLO'

>>>

'-' * 60

'-- -----------

>>>

60

* '-'

'-- -----------

substring = '=' + '-' * 3 + '=' '10' * 5 + 4 * substring

2 * '12' + '.' + '3' * 3 + 'e-' + 4 * '76'

Identify regularities in the following strings, and write expressions that, starting from shorter substrings and using the concatenation and repetition operators, produce the strings shown. Enter variables to form the expressions when you consider it appropriate.

'%%%%%. /. /. / <-> <->'

```
'(@) (@) (@) ====== (@) (@) (@) ======'
'asdfasdfasdf = - = - = - = - = - = - ?????? asdfasdf'
'........ ***** ___ ***** ___........ ***** ___ ***** ___'
```

....

Other types of data

Python has a rich set of data types. Some, such as structured data types, will be studied in detail later. However, and given the introductory nature of this text, we will not study in detail two other basic types: integer ((long)) numbers and complex numbers. We will simply present them succinctly.

The range of floating numbers may be insufficient for certain applications. Python offers the possibility of working with numbers with an arbitrarily long number of numbers: the integers ((long)). A long integer always ends with the letter L. Here are some examples of long integers: 1L, -52L, 1237645272817635341571828374645L. Integer numbers automatically promote long integers when necessary.

```
>>>
2 ** 30
1073741824
>>>
2 ** 31
2147483648L
```

Look at the ((L)) that appears at the end of the second result: although 2 and 31 are integers ((normal)), the result of evaluating 2 ** 31 is a long integer. This is because normal integers are encoded in complement to 2 of 32 bits, and 2 ** 31 cannot be represented in complement to 2 of 32 bits.

While long integers are comfortable because they never produce overflow errors, you should keep in mind that they are very inefficient: they occupy (much) more memory than normal ones and operate with them is (much) slower.

Finally, Python also offers the possibility of working with complex numbers. A pure complex number always ends with the letter j, which represents the value −1. A complex number with real part is expressed by adding the real part to a pure complex. Here are examples of complex numbers: 4j, 1 + 2j, 2.0 + 3j, 1 - 0.354j.

The concept of comparison between numbers is familiar to you because you have studied it before in mathematics. Python extends the concept of comparison to other types of data, such as strings. In the case of the operators == and! = The meaning is clear: two strings are equal if they are equal character to character, and different otherwise. But what does it mean that one chain is smaller than another? Python uses a very natural string comparison criterion: the alphabetical order. In principle, a string is smaller than another if it precedes it when arranged in a dictionary. For example, 'below' is less than 'above'.

And how do strings compare with non-alphabetic characters? That is, is '@@' less than or greater than 'abc'? Python uses the

ASCII codes of the characters to decide their alphabetical order (see tables in Appendix A). To know the numerical value that corresponds to a character, you can use the predefined ord function, to which you must pass the character in question as an argument.

ord ('a')

2.6 Predefined Functions

The inverse function (the one that passes a number to its equivalent character) is chr.

chr (97)

The ASCII table presents a problem when we want to order words: the uppercase letters have a lower numerical value than the lower case letters (so 'Shoe' precedes 'garlic') and the accented letters are always ((greater)) than its unstressed equivalents ('abanico' is less than ''abaco'). There are ways to configure the operating system to take into account the ordering criteria of each language when making comparisons, but that is another story. If you want to know M'as, read the table entitled ((C'odigo ASCII yc'odigo ISOLATINO-1)) and see the ap'endice A.

ASCII code and IsoLatin-1 code

In the early days of computers, characters were encoded using 6 or 7 bits. Each computer used a different character encoding, so there were compatibility issues: it was not easy to transport data from one computer to another. The Americans defined a standard 7-bit coding that assigned a character to each number between 0 and 127: the ASCII table (from the American Standard Code for Information Interchange). This table (which you can consult in an appendix) only contained the characters commonly used in the English language. The ASCII table was subsequently enriched by defining an 8-bit code for Western European languages: the IsoLatin-1 table, also known as ISO-8859-1 (there are other tables for other languages). This table matches the ASCII table in its first 128 characters and adds all the symbols commonly used in the languages of Western Europe. A standardized variant is the ISO-8859-15 table, which is ISO-8859-1 enriched with the Euro symbol.

We have studied the basic arithmetic operators. Python also provides functions that we can use in expressions. These functions are said to be predefined. The abs function, for example, calculates the absolute value of a number. We can use it as in these expressions:

abs (-3)

3

abs (3)

3

The number on which the function is applied is called an argument. Note that the argument of the function must be enclosed in parentheses:

Predefined because we can also define our own functions. We will arrive.

abs (0)

0

abs 0

File "<stdin>", line 1

abs 0

^

SyntaxError: invalid syntax

There are many predefined functions, but it is soon to learn them all. We summarize some that you can already use:

float: conversion to floating. If it receives an integer number as an argument, it returns the same number converted to an equivalent float.

float (3)

3.0

The float function also accepts string arguments. When a string is passed, float converts it into the floating number that it represents:

>>>

float ('3.2')

3.2

```
>>>
float ('3.2e10')
32000000000.0
```

But if the string does not represent a float, an error of type ValueError occurs, that is, ((value error)):

```
>>> float ('a text')
Traceback (innermost last):
File "<stdin>", line 1, in?
ValueError: invalid literal for float (): a text
```

If float receives a floating argument, it returns the same value that is supplied as an argument.

int: conversion to whole. If it receives a floating number as an argument, it returns the integer obtained by eliminating the fractional part.

```
>>> int (2.1)
2
>>> int (-2.9)
-2
```

Also, the int function accepts as argument a string:

```
int ('2')
2
```

If int receives an entire argument, it returns the argument as is.

str: conversion to chain. Receive a number and return a representation of this as a string.

```
>>>
```

str (2.1)

'2.1'

>>> str (234E47)

'2.34e + 49'

The rounding of int can be up or down depending on the computer on which you run it. This is because int relies on the behavior of the automatic rounding of C (the Python interpreter we use is written in C) and its behavior is undefined. If you want a homogeneous rounding behavior, then use the round, floor or ceil functions, which are explained below.

2.7 Functions Defined In Modules

The str function can also receive a string as an argument, but in that case, it returns the same string.

round: rounding. It can be used with one or two arguments. If used with only one argument, round the number to the nearest floating whose decimal part is null.

>>> round (2.1)

2.0

>>> round (2.9)

3.0

>>> round (-2.9)

-3.0

>>>

round (2)

2.0

(Note that the result is always of the floating type!) If round receives two arguments, these must be separated by a comma and the second indicates the number of decimals we want to keep after rounding.

These functions (and those we will study later) can be part of expressions and their arguments can, in turn, be expressions. Look at the following examples:

>>>abs (-23)% int (7.3)

>>>abs (round (-34.2765,1))

34.3

>>> str (float (str (2) * 3 + '.123')) + '321' 222.123321

. . . . exercises. . . . . . .

. . . .

27 Calculate with a single expression the absolute rounding value of −3.2. (The result is 3.0.)

28 Convert (into a single expression) to a string the result of the 5011/10000 division rounded to 3 decimal places.

29 What results from evaluating these expressions?

      str (2.1) + str (1.2)

      int (str (2) + str (3))

      str (int (12.3)) + 'o'

      int ('2' + '3')

str (2 + 3)
str (int (2.1) + float (3))

2.7. Functions defined in modules

Python also provides trigonometric functions, logarithms, etc., but they are not directly available when we start a session. Before using them we must indicate to Python that we are going to do it. To do this, we import each function of a module.

48 Introduction to Python Programming

c 2003 Andr´es Marzal and Isabel Gracia 2 An advanced calculator

2.7.1. The math module

We will start by importing the sine function (without, of the English ((sinus))) of the mathematical module (math):

>>> from math import without

Now we can use the function in our calculations:

without (0)

0.0

without (1)

0.841470984808

Note that the sine function argument must be expressed in radians.

Initially Python does not ((know)) calculate the sine function. When we import a function, Python ((learns)) its definition and allows us to use it. Function definitions reside in modules. Trigonometric functions reside in the mathematical module. For example, the cosine function, at this time, is unknown to Python.

```
cos (0)
Traceback (innermost last):
File "<stdin>", line 1, in?
NameError: cos
```

Before using it, it is necessary to import it from the mathematical module:

```
from math import cos
cos (0)
1.0
```

In the same sentence we can import more than one function. Simply separate their names with commas:

```
>>> from math import sin, cos
```

It can be tedious to import a large number of functions and variables from a module. Python offers a shortcut: if we use an asterisk, all the elements of a module are imported. To import all the functions of the math module we write:

```
>>> from math import *
```

That easy. Anyway, it is not very advisable for two reasons:

When importing element by element, the program gains in readability, because we know where each identifier comes from.

If we have defined a variable with a specific name and that name coincides with that of a function defined in a module, our variable will be replaced by the function. If you do not know all the elements that define a module, it is possible that this coincidence of name takes place, it initially went unnoticed and you get a surprise when you try to use the variable.

Here is an example of the second of the problems indicated:

```
pow = 1
from math import *
pow + = 1
```

Traceback (most recent call last):

File "<stdin>", line 1, in?

TypeError: unsupported operand type (s) for + =: 'builtin_function_or_method' and ' int'

2.7 Functions defined in modules

2006/09 / 25-15: 31

Avoiding coincidences

Python offers a way to avoid the problem of coincidences: import only the module.

import math

In this way, all the functions of the math module are available, but using the module name and a period as a prefix:

```
>>>import math
>>>print math.sin (0)
```

Python complains that we try to add an integer and a function. Indeed, there is a pow function in the math module. When importing all the content of math, our variable has been ((crushed)) by the function.

30 What results will be obtained when evaluating the following Python expressions? First calculate the resulting value of each expression by hand and check, with the help of the computer, if your result is correct.

int (exp (2 * log (3)))

round (4 * sin (3 * pi / 2))

abs (log10 (.01) * sqrt (25))

round (3.21123 * log10 (1000), 3)

2.7.2. Other modules of interest

There is a large number of modules, each of them specialized in a specific field of application. Precisely, one of the reasons why Python is a powerful and extremely useful language is because of the large collection of modules with which it is distributed. Ha and modules for web application design, user interface design, data compression, cryptography, multimedia, etc. And new modules are constantly appearing: any Python programmer can create their own modules, thus adding functions that simplify programming in any given environment and making them available to others. programmers We will limit ourselves to presenting you now a few functions of a couple of interesting modules.

Float Accuracy

We have said that the arguments of trigonometric functions must be expressed in radians. As you know, sen (π) = 0. Let's see what Python thinks:

from math import sin, pi

without (pi)

1.2246063538223773e-16

The result provided by Python is not zero, but a number very close to zero: 0.00000000000000012246063538223773. Was Python wrong? Not quite. We have said before that floating numbers have limited accuracy. The number π is defined in the mathematical module as 3.1415926535897931, when in fact it has an infinite number of decimals. Thus, we have not asked for exactly the calculation of the sine of π, but that of a next number, but not exactly the same. On the other hand, the mathematical module makes calculations using algorithms that can introduce errors in the result.

We go with another important module: sys (system), the module of ((system)) (sys is an abbreviation of English ((system))). This module contains functions that access the operating system and computer dependent constants. An important function is exit, which immediately aborts the execution of the interpreter (in English means ((exit))). The maxint variable, also defined in sys, contains the largest integer number that can be worked with, and the version variable, indicates which Python version we are working with:

```
>>>from sys import maxint, version
>>>maxint
2147483647
>>>version
'2.3 (# 1, Aug 2 2003, 09:00:57) \ n [GCC 3.3]'
```

eye! With this we do not want to tell you that the version function or the maxint predefined value is important and that you must learn its name and purpose by heart, but that Python modules contain hundreds of useful functions for different tasks. A good Python programmer knows how to deal with the modules. There is a reference manual that describes all the standard Python modules. You will find it with the Python documentation under the name ((Library reference)) (in English means ((library reference))) and you could consult it with a web browser. 8 .

2.8. Methods

Data of certain types allow to invoke special functions: the so-called ((methods)).

Of those we already know, only chains allow methods to be invoked on them.

A method allows, for example, to obtain a lowercase version of the string on which it is invoked:

```
string = 'An EXAMPLE of String'
  string.lower ()
'an example string'
>>>'ANOTHER EXAMPLE' .lower ()
'another example'
```

The syntax is different from that of a conventional function call. The first thing that appears is the object itself on which the call is made. The method name is separated from the object with a period. Open and closed parentheses at the end are mandatory.

There is another method, upper (((uppercase)), in English, means ((uppercase))), which changes all characters to uppercase.

In a Linux installation you will usually find it in the URL file: /usr/doc/python/html/index.html (Note: in SuSE, file: / usr / share / doc / packages / python / html / index .html). If you are working on a computer with Internet access, try http://www.python.org/python/doc/2.2/lib/lib.html .

```
        'Another example'.upper ()
'ANOTHER EXAMPLE'
```

And another, title that passes the initial of each word to uppercase. You will ask yourself what this last function may be worth. Imagine that you have made a data collection program that makes a census of people and that each individual personally enters their name on the computer. It is very likely that some will use only uppercase and others uppercase and lowercase. If we apply title to each of the names, they will all end up in a unique format:

'PEDRO F. MAS'.title ()' Pedro F. Mas'

'Juan CANO'.title ()

'Juan Cano'

Some methods accept parameters. The replace method, for example, receives two strings as an argument: a pattern and a replacement. The method searches for the pattern in the chain on which the method is invoked and replaces all its occurrences with the replacement chain.

'a small example'. replace ('small', 'large') 'a great example'

a_string = 'abc'.replace (' b ',' - ')

a chain

'a-c'

`As we present new types of data and deepen our knowledge of the chains, you will learn new methods.

Strings, methods and the string module

String methods were n module functions in older versions of Python.

To pass a string to uppercase, for example, you had to do the following:

    from string import upper

    upper ('Another example')

'ANOTHER EXAMPLE'

And you can still do it that way, although it is more convenient to use methods. The string module continues to offer these functions to ensure the compatibility of programs written long ago with the new Python versions.

WHY SHOULD I LEARN PYTHON?

Python is presented as the programming language best valued by programmers and most sought after by companies. As extracted from the Stackoverflow 2018 report, the international development information dissemination platform, Python remains unstoppable. Within the section of the most valued programming languages, in 2018, it has surpassed C # in popularity! It should be remembered that in 2017 it already surpassed PHP, so it continues to gain positions.

What Is Python?

Python was born in the late eighties by the Dutchman Guido van Rossum, but it was not until the 1990s that it took shape and was published in version 0.9.0. A curiosity? Its name comes from its creator's fondness for Monty Python, the group of British comedians.

What best characterizes Python is that it is a multiparadigma programming language; that is, programmers have to use a particular style of programming, since it allows several styles at once: object-oriented programming, imperative programming and functional programming. Other paradigms are supported through the use of extensions. As you can see, it would be a mix of styles that make it unique.

Advantages of Python

Returning back to the Stackover report, where languages are scored and positioned in categories such as "loved", "feared" or "desired", Python appears as the language with the best prospects for being the third to be more "Loved" and the first to be "desired."

Although it is still far from top languages such as Java or SQL, Python is highly valued and is considered a safe value in the future. In addition, it is built on very interesting bases. Let's review some of them!

Python is a multiplatform It is an interpreted programming language; and because of this, it works in any type of system that integrates its interpreter. A big advantage.

Free and open source Anyone can contribute to its development and dissemination. It is managed by the Python Software Foundation, a non-profit organization; and therefore, you do not have to pay any license to distribute software developed with this language. We like this in the 21st century!

Highly valued by large companies Google, Walt Disney, NASA, Yahoo!, Facebook or YouTube Nokia use Python to develop their products and services. As you can see, it can be used in various types of sectors, regardless of your business activity.

Very productive language Python is powerful, flexible and its syntax is clear and concise.

Why Should I Learn To Program With Python?

As you have seen, there are many features of this language to make it very desired and valued. In addition, learning Python you will understand the basics of programming and it will be very easy to go from programming with one language or another.

You don't need to have any basis to start from scratch with Python. Also don't worry if you don't like math or think you're not good at technical problems, Python has a very elegant and clean syntax, which will allow you to progress.

If you are interested in becoming aware of what programming means, Python is the ideal language.

Advantages of Programming with Python

Are you a programmer? Surely on some occasion you had to use Python or even, it is the language you like most today and the one you use for your work. It does not matter, the fact is that this tool is available to many programmers in the world and therefore, it has a great list of advantages of programming with Python that we will leave you detailed here:

Massive Use

Spaces like GitHub, has a large number of projects that You can use it again and these are made in this language, so it allows you a wide range of around 95,000 in this community.

Beginner Use

Being one of the slowest languages, it is within reach of those who are just beginning so you can take it easy and with the smallest detail. While it is not the simplest or didactic language, it does allow you to carry everything with ease.

Income

Programmers who use this language, can have an income of up to $ 110,000 a year, an interesting package for the world economy and more when taking into account that these data come from the 2015-2016 exercise according to the data collected by Dice, that is, at present, the same may be greater.

Packages

MatplotlibBasemap and Seaborn are some of the pluggins or Python packages has in its structure, enabling increased efficiency when generating information and design of the project itself,well as the organization offering have these aggregates.

Simple

It offers a pattern for programming and based on it, you are responsible for generating the necessary information, so the time and ease of delivery are in your hands thanks to the use of this program.

Practical

Each of the libraries that are necessary to program in Python, you should not look for them outside, since the program itself locates them in its database to make things easier.

Inclusion

The changes and updates of the language are commented and consulted by the community of its use, so it is simple that it remains true to its style and also, everything that changes or includes is in the necessary order.

These advantages could be enough to convince you, in the same way, we invite you to try the language and be aware of every detail it offers, as well as its disadvantages.

Chapter 3

Programs

"Dear, I really have to get a thinner pencil!" I can't handle this at all: write all kinds of things, without my dictating them.

Lewis Carroll, Alice through the mirror.

So far we have used Python in an interactive environment: we have introduced expressions (and assignments to variables) and Python has evaluated them and provided their respective results immediately.

But using the system only in this way greatly limits our ability to work. In this topic we will learn to introduce sequences of expressions and assignments in a text file and ask Python to execute them all, one after another. We will call the content of the text file 1 program .

You can generate the files with any text editor. We will use a programming environment: the PythonG environment. A programming environment is a set of tools that facilitate the work of the programmer.

3.1. The PythonG

The PythonG programming environment is a program written in Python useful for writing your Python programs. You will find the PythonG program at http://marmota.act.uji.es/MTP . Once you have installed it, run the pythong.py program. A window will appear on the screen . You can enter expressions in the

121

PythonG interactive environment, just as we did when executing the python interpreter from a terminal.

Let's not take longer and write our first program. In the File menu there is an option called New. When selected, an editing window is created that replaces the interactive environment. Between the window and the menu a tab will appear with the text <anonymous>. You can return to the interactive interpreter at any time by clicking on the <python> tab. Type the following text in the <anonymous> 2 window :

<anonymous>

```
from math import pi
radius = 1
perimeter = 2 * pi * radius
perimeter
```

Save the text you have written in a file called myprogram.py by selecting the Save option from the File menu.

Python programs are also often called scripts.

2 You should not type the line numbers that appear in the left margin of the programs. We put them only to facilitate subsequent references to their lines.

3.2 The PythonG environment

The PythonG programming environment. In the upper area a menu bar appears. Under it, on the left, a work area in which a Python interactive environment is shown. In the right area there are two boxes: the upper one is a drawing area and the lower one is an input / output console for Python programs. The button with the letter ((G)) allows you to hide / show the area of graphic output.

myiprogram 4.py myiprogram.py

```
from math import pi
radius = 1
perimeter = 2 * pi * radius
perimeter
```

The Run / Abort option in the Python menu allows you to run the program: select it. What happen? Any. Although the program has been run, we don't see the result anywhere.

Py point

There is an agreement whereby files containing Python programs have a py extension in their name. The extension of a file name are the characters of the same that happen to the (last) point. A file called example.py has a py extension.

The idea of extensions comes from old and is a mere agreement. You can do without it, but it is not convenient. In graphic environments (such as KDE, Gnome or Microsoft Windows) the extension is used to determine which icon is associated with the file and what application must be started to open the file when clicking (or double-clicking)) in the same.

Let's analyze the program step by step. The first line of myprogram.py does not produce any output: it is limited to importing the variable pi. The second line is blank. Blank lines only serve to make the program more readable by separating different parts of it. The third defines a variable called radius and assigns it the value 1, and we already saw that the assignments

They do not produce a visible result on the screen. The fourth line is also an assignment. The fifth line is blank and the last one is an expression (although very simple). When an expression appeared on a line, the interactive environment showed the result of its evaluation. However, the same does not happen now that we work with a program. This is an important difference between the interactive use of Python and the execution of programs: the evaluation of expressions does not produce screen output in a program. So how will we see the results that our programs produce? We must learn to use a new sentence: print (in English, ((print))). In principle, it is used in this way:

print expression and write on screen the result of evaluating the expression.

We modify the program so that it reads like this:

myprogram.py myprogram.py

```
    from math import pi
```

radius = 1

perimeter = 2 * pi * radius

 perimeter print

Keys

Text editor that integrates PythonG environment can be handled very sencill way to

with the mouse. Many of the orders you can give by selecting the corresponding menu option have a keyboard shortcut, that is, a key combination that allows you to execute the order without having to take the mouse, move to the menu bar, keep the mouse pressed (or click) on one of them and release the mouse (or click again) on the option associated with the order. If you get used to using keyboard shortcuts, you will be much more productive. Memorizing them costs a lot of effort at first, but the rewards in the medium and long term.

We summarize here the keyboard shortcuts for the different orders. Some shortcuts require the pressing of four keys, well, of two groups of two keys that are pressed simultaneously. For example, to open a file you have to press Cx and then Cf. A double sequence like that will be indicated like this: Cx Cf.

New file

Cx Cn

Open file

Cx Cf

save

Cx Cs

Save as

Cx Cw

Close

Cx k

Get out

Cx Cc

Undo

Cz

Redo

CMz

Cut

Cx

Copy

DC

Paste

Hp

Look for

Cs

Replace

Esc%

Go to line number

Esc g

Increase font size

C- +

Reduce font size

C--

Run program

Cc Cc

Abort Execution

Cc Cc

(Esc represents the keyboard of ((escape)) (the key in the upper left corner on the keyboard)

and M (in CMz) to the Alt key, although it is the initial of the term ((meta)).)

There are other combinations of keys that are very useful and whose orders are not accessible through a menu. Here you have them:

Go to beginning of line

AC

Go to end of line

EC

Forward word

C- →

Turn a word back

C- ←

Select

S- <cursor key>

(S is the úppercase key, which in English is called ((shift)).)

If you are now equating the program, the result will appear in the lower right box. This box shows the output of any print statement.

31 Design a program that, based on the value of the side of a square (3 meters), shows the value of its perimeter (in meters) and that of its area (in square meters).

(The perimeter should give you 12 meters and the area 9 square meters.)

32 Design a program that, based on the value of the base and the height of a triangle (3 and 5 meters, respectively), shows the value of its area (in square meters).

Remember that the area 'A of a triangle can be calculated from the base b and the height h as A = 1 2 bh.

You can use any text editor to write Python programs. Be careful! You should not use a word processor, that is, the text should not be formatted (font changes, font sizes, etc.). Applications such as Microsoft Word do format the text. The Microsoft Windows notebook, for example, is an appropriate text editor for programming (although very poor).

In Unix there is a great variety of text editors. The most used are the vi and the Emacs (or its XEmacs variant). If you have to use a text editor, we recommend the latter. XEmacs incorporates a Python work mode (python-mode) that greatly facilitates the writing of Python programs.

PythonG key combinations have been defined to make working with XEmacs easy, as they are basically identical. That way, you won't find it difficult to alternate between PythonG and XEmacs. Once you have written a program it is possible to execute it directly, without entering the PythonG environment. If you invoke the python interpreter followed by the name of a file from the line of

Unix orders, a session with the interactive interpreter will not be initiated, but the program contained in the file in question will be executed.

For example, if we execute the python miprograma.py command in the command line, we have the following result:

python myprogram.py

6,28318530718

Then the prompt of the interpreter of Unix orders will appear again asking us for new orders.

3.3. Entrance exit

The programs we have seen in the previous section suffer from a serious inconvenience: every time you want to obtain results for different data you should edit the text file that contains the program.

For example, the following program calculates the volume of a sphere from its radius, which is one meter:

volume sphere 8.py volume sphere.py

```
from math import pi
radius = 1
volume = 4.0 / 3.0 * pi * radio ** 3
print volume
```
Here you have the result of running the program:

```
python volume_sphere.py
```
4.18879020479

If you want to calculate now the volume of a sphere of 3 meters of radius, you must edit the file that contains the program, going to the third line and changing it so that the program becomes this:

volume sphere 9.py volume sphere.py

```
from math import pi
```
3 radius = 3

```
volume = 4.0 / 3.0 * pi * radio ** 3
print volume
```
Now we can axis cutar the program:

```
python volume_sphere.py 113.097335529
```
And if you now want to calculate the volume for another radio, start over: open the file with the text editor, go to the third line, modify the value of the radio and save the file. It is not the height of comfort.

We will learn to make our program, when it is executed, ask for the value of the radius for which we are going to make the calculations without having to edit the program file.

There is a predefined function, raw_input (in English means ((raw input))), which does the following: it stops the execution of the program and waits for the user to write a text (the

Implicit execution of the interpreter

It is not necessary to explicitly call the Python interpreter to run the programs. In Unix there is an agreement that allows you to call the interpreter automatically: if the first line of the text file begins with the characters #!, It is assumed that, then, the path in which to find the interpreter that we want to use to execute the file.

If, for example, our Python interpreter is in / usr / local / bin / pyth on, the following file:

myiprogram 5.py myiprogram.py

```
#! / usr / local / bin / python
from math import pi
    radius = 1
    perimeter = 2 * pi * radius
    perimeter print
```

In addition to containing the program, it would allow the Python interpreter to be automatically invoked. Or almost. We would miss one last step: give the file permission to execute. If you want to give permission to execute, you must use the Unix chmod command. For example,

$ chmod u + x my program. py

gives execution permission to the user who owns the file. From now on, to execute the program we will only have to write the name of the file:

    myprogram.py

6,28318530718

If you want to practice, generate executable files for the programs of the last three exercises.

Keep in mind that sometimes this procedure fails. On different systems Python may be installed in different directories. It may be more practical to replace the first line with this one:

My program 6.py My program.py

```
#! / usr / bin / env python
from math import pi
    radius = 1
    perimeter = 2 * pi * radius
    perimeter print
```

The env program (which should be in / usr / bin on any system) takes care of ((search))

The program loves Python.

radio value, for example) and press the carriage return key; at that time the execution continues and the function returns a string with the text that the user typed.

If you want the radius to be a floating value, you must transform the string returned by raw_input into a floating type data by calling the float function. The float function would receive as an argument the string returned by raw_input and provide a floating point number. (Remember, when you need it, that there is another conversion function, int, that returns an integer instead of a float.) On the other hand, raw_input is a function and therefore the use of the parentheses that follow his name is mandatory, even when he has no arguments.

```
from math import pi
radius = 1
perimeter = 2 * pi * radius
perimeter print
```

The env program (which should be in / usr / bin on any system) takes care of ((search)). The program loves Python, radio value, for example and press the carriage return key; at that time the execution continues and the function returns a string with the text that the user typed.

If you want the radius to be a floating value, you must transform the string returned by raw input into a floating type data by calling the float function. The float function would receive as an argument the string returned by raw input and provide a floating point number. (Remember, when you need it, that there is another conversion function, int, that returns an integer instead of a float.) On the other hand, raw input is a function and therefore the use of the parentheses that follow his name is mandatory, even when he has no arguments.

Here is the new program:

volume sphere 10.py volume sphere.py

from math import pi

le_text 0 = raw_input ()

radius = float (read_text)

volume = 4.0 / 3.0 * pi * radio ** 3

print volume

This other version is shorter:

volume sphere 11.py volume sphere.py

from math import pi

radius = float (raw_input ())

volume = 4.0 / 3.0 * pi * radio ** 3

print volume

When executing the program from the Unix command line, the computer appears to be locked. It is not: Python is actually requesting a keyboard input and expects it to be provided by the user. If you type, for example, number 3 and press the carriage return key, Python responds by printing the value 113.097335529 on the screen. You can rerun the program and, instead of typing number 3, type any other value; Python will answer us with the value of the volume of the sphere for a radius equal to the value that you have typed.

But the program is not very elegant, because it leaves the computer locked until the user types an amount and does not report what exactly that amount is. We are going to make the program indicate, by means of a message, what data you want to be typed. The raw input function accepts an argument: a string with the message to display.

Modify the program so that it looks like this:

volume sphere 12. py volume sphere.py

```
from math import pi
radius = float (raw_input ( 'Give me the radius:' ))
volume = 4.0 / 3.0 * pi * radio ** 3
print volume
```

Now, every time you run it, it will show the message on the screen ((Give me the radio :)) and it will stop its execution until you enter a number and press the carriage return.

python volume_sphere.py Give me the radius: 3 113.097335529

The way of using the program from PythonG is very similar. When you run the program, the message ((Give me the radio :)) appears in the input / output console and the execution is stopped. The user must enter the value of the radio, which appears on the console itself, and press the carriage return key at the end. The result appears below in the console.

3.3.2. More about the print statement

Strings can also be used to display texts by size at any time through print statements.

volume sphere 13.py volume sphere.py

```
from math import pi
```

```
print 'Program for calculating the volume of a sphere.'
radius = float (raw_input ('Give me the radius:'))
volume = 4.0 / 3.0 * pi * radio ** 3
print volume
print 'Thank you for using this program.'
```

When you run this program, notice that the strings shown with print do not appear in quotes. The user of the program is not interested in knowing that we are showing data of the string type: he is only interested in the text of these chains. Much better, then, do not show the quotes.

A print statement can show more than one result on the same line: it is enough to separate all the values we want to display with commas. Each of the commas is translated into a space of separation n. The following program:

```
volume sphere 14.py volume sphere.py
from math import pi
print 'Program for calculating the volume of a sphere.'
radius = float (raw_input ('Give me the radius (in meters):'))
volume = 4.0 / 3.0 * pi * radio ** 3
print 'Dial volume:', volume, 'cubic meters'
```

This causes the text to be displayed ((Volume of the sphere :)), followed by the value of the variable volume and ending with ((cubic meters)). Note that the elements of the last print are separated from each other by blank spaces:

Program for the calculation of the volume of a sphere.

Give me the radius (in meters): 2

The volume of the sphere is 33.5103216383 cubic meters

Apparently so far, each print starts printing on a new line. We can avoid it if the previous print ends in a comma. Look at this program:

volume sphere.py volume sphere.py

```
from math import pi
print 'Prog branch for the calculation of the volume of a sphere.'
radius = float (raw_input ('Give me the radius (in meters):'))
volume = 4.0 / 3.0 * pi * radio ** 3
print 'Dial volume:',
print volume, 'cubic meters'
```

The penultimate line is a print statement that ends in a comma. If we execute the program we will obtain a result that is absolutely equivalent to that of the previous version:

Program for the calculation of the volume of a sphere.

Give me the radio (in meters):

The volume of the radio is 33.5103216383 cubic meters

It happens that each print prints, in principle, a special character called ((new line)), which causes the cursor (the position in which the output is written on the screen at every moment) to move to The next line. If print ends in a comma,

Python does not print the character ((new line)), so the cursor does not move to the next line. The next print, then, will print immediately below, on the same line.

3.3.3. Formatted output

With the print statement we can control the appearance of the output to some extent. But we don't have total control:

Each comma in the print statement causes a blank space to appear on the screen. What if we don't want that blank space to appear?

Each number occupies as many ((boxes)) of the screen as characters it has. For example, number 2 occupies a square, and number 2000, four. What if we want all numbers to occupy the same number of boxes?

Python allows us to control the output on the screen with absolute precision. For this we have to learn a new use of the% operator. Study this program carefully.

3.5. Graphics

All the programs that we have presented to you use the keyboard and the screen in ((text mode)) to interact with the user. However, you are used to interacting with the computer through a graphic terminal and using, in addition to the keyboard, the mouse. In this section, we will briefly introduce the graphical capabilities of the PythonG environment. Appendix B summarizes the functions we present in this and other sections.

Start the PythonG environment and you will see that there is a blank square in the upper right area. It is the graphic window or canvas. All graphic elements that your programs produce will be displayed on it. The lower left corner of the graphic window has coordinates (0, 0), and the upper right corner coordinates (1000, 1000).

Our first graphic program is very simple: draw a line on the canvas that goes from point (100, 100) to point (900, 900). The create_line function draws a line on the screen. You must provide four numerical values: the coordinates of the starting point and the end point of the line:

a straight line and a straight line

create_line (100,100, 900,900)

Run the program.

In addition to straight lines, you can draw other graphic elements. Here is a list of the graphic element creation functions offered by PythonG:

create_point (x, y): draw a point on (x, y).

 (x, y)

create_line (x1, y1, x2, y2): draw a line from (x1, y1) to (x2, y2).

(x 2 , y 2)

(x 1 , y 1)

create_circle (x, y, radius): draw a circle with center at (x, y) and radius r.

create_rectangle (x1, y1, x2, y2) : draw a rectangle with opposite corners at (x1, y1) and (x2, y2).

(x 2 , y 2)

(x 1 , y 1)

create_text (x, y, string, size, anchor): draw the string text at the point (x, y).

The size parameter expresses the font size in points. A reasonable value for the sources is 10 or 12 points. The last parameter, anchor, indicates whether the text is ((anchor)) to the point (x, y) by the center ('CENTER'), by the upper left corner ('NW'), lower left (' SW '), etc.

'N'

'CENTER'

'NW'

'NE'

'W' An anchored chain 'E'

'SW' 'S' 'SE'

For example, create_text (100, 100, 'Hello', 10, 'NE') draws the text ((Hello)) on the screen by anchoring the upper right corner in the coordinates (100, 100).

(100, 100)

Hello

create_filled_circle (x, y, radius) : draw a filled circle (black) with a center at (x, y) and radius r.

create_filled_rectangle (x1, y1, x2, y2): draw a filled rectangle (black) with opposite corners at (x1, y1) and (x2, y2).

The three concentric circles have radii 100, 200 and 300, respectively.

You should know that all graphic element creation functions accept an optional parameter: a string that can take the value 'white' (white), 'black' (black), 'red' (red), 'blue' (blue), 'green' (green), 'yellow' (yellow), 'cyan' or 'magenta'. With that parameter, the color of the element is indicated. If omitted, it takes the default value 'black'.

We are going to make a first program with graphic output and that presents a certain utility: a program that shows the percentage of suspensions, approved, notable and outstanding of a subject by means of a ((pie chart)) . Here is an example of a graph like the one we want for a 10% suspension rate, 20% approved, 40% notable and 30% outstanding:

Apr (20%)

Sus (10%)

Not (40%)

Sob (30%)

Let us begin. The circle is easy: it will have a center at (500, 500) and its radius will be 500 units. This way we get it to occupy the largest possible screen ratio.

8.py cake.py cake

create_circle (500,500, 500)

Better we will relatively independent the center and radio program of the circumference.

Inc:

9.py cake.py cake

x = 500

y = 500

radius = 500

create_circle (x, y, radius)

Thus, changing the location or size of the pie chart will be simple. Let's keep going. We are going to draw the cut of the people who have suspended. We have to draw two lines. The horizontal line is very simple: part of (x, y) and reaches (x + radius, y):

10.py cake.py cake

x = 500

y = 500

radius = 500

create_circle (x, y , radius)

create_line (x, y, x + radius, y)

The second line is more complicated. What coordinates does the point (x_1, y_1) have:

(x_1, y_1)

α

(x, y)

Radius r

A little trigonometry would suit us. If we knew the angle, the calculation would be simple:

x 1 = x + radius cos (α)

y 1 = y + radius sin (α)

The angle represents the portion of the circle that corresponds to the suspensions. Like the full conference of a circle runs at an angle of 2π radians, and the suspense constituting 10% of the total, the angle α is $2\pi \cdot 10/100$ or, to be clearer, $2\pi \cdot$ suspense / 100.

11.py cake.py cake

```
from math import sin, cos, pi
x = 500
y = 500
radius = 500
suspense = 10
approved = 20
notables = 40
outstanding = 30
create_circle (x, y, radio)
create_line (x, y, x + radius, y)
alpha = 2 * pi * suspense / 100
create_line (x, y, x + radio * cos (alpha), y + radio * sin (alpha))
```

It is done. In passing, we have prepared variables to store the percentage of suspensions, approvals, etc.

Let's go to the next line, which corresponds to the approved ones. What value does the angle β have? If we know it, it is immediate to know x 2 and 2 :

(x 2 , y 2)

β

(x, y)

Radius

You might think that if α was calculated as $2\pi \cdot$ suspense / 100, β would be $2\pi \cdot$ approved / 100. But you are wrong. The angle β does not represent 20% of the circumference, but 30%, which is the result of adding approvals and suspensions:

= 2π (suspenses + approved) / 100

from math import sin, cos, pi

x = 500

y = 500

radius = 500

suspense = 10

approved = 20

notables = 40

envelopes before = 30

create_circle (x, y, radio)

create_line (x, y, x + radius, y)

alpha = 2 * pi * suspense / 100

create_line (x, y, x + radio * cos (alpha), y + radio * sin (alpha))

beta = 2 * pi * (suspensions + approved) / 100

create_line (x, y, x + radio * cos (beta), y + radio * sin (beta))

We are going to let you complete the program yourself including the numbers and over-outlets. We will end up presenting, yes, the way we put the legends that indicate to which each part of the cake corresponds. We want to label the first fragment like this:

sus (10%)

We will use the create_text function. We need to determine the coordinates of the center of the text, which falls in the center right of the pie portion that corresponds to the suspense.

α / 2

The point has coordinates (0.5 radius cos (α / 2), 0.5 radius sin (α / 2)):

from math import sin, cos, pi

x = 500

y = 500

radius = 500

suspense = 10

approved = 20

notables = 40

outstanding = 30

create_circle (x, y, radio)

create_line (x, y, x + radius, y)

alpha = 2 * pi * suspense / 100

create_line (x, y, x + radio * cos (alpha), y + radio * sin (alpha))

create_text (x + .5 * radio * cos (alpha / 2), and + .5 * radio * sin (alpha / 2), 'sus (% d %%)' % suspended)

beta = 2 * pi * (suspensions + approved) / 100

create_line (x, y, x + radio * cos (beta), y + radio * sin (beta))

And the legend of the approved? What coordinates does its center have? Look closely at how much the angle that determines its position is worth:

$\alpha + (\beta - \alpha) / 2$

It is done:

from math import sin, cos, pi

x = 500

y = 500

radius = 500

suspense = 10

approved = 20

notables = 40

outstanding = 30

create te_circle (x, y, radius)

create_line (x, y, x + radius, y)

alpha = 2 * pi * suspense / 100

create_line (x, y, x + radio * cos (alpha), y + radio * sin (alpha))

create_text (x + .5 * radio * cos (alpha / 2), and + .5 * radio * sin (alpha / 2), 'sus (% d %%)'% suspended)

```
beta = 2 * pi * (suspensions + approved) / 100
create_line (x, y, x + radio * cos (beta), y + radio * sin (beta))
create_text (x + .5 * radio * cos (alpha + (beta-alpha) / 2), \
and + .5 * radio * sin (alpha + (beta-alpha) / 2), 'apr (% d %%)'%
approved
```

Look at line 20. It ends in a backslash and the sentence continues on line 21. It is a way of telling Python that the sentence is too long for it to be comfortable or legible to arrange it in one line and, therefore, continues on the next line. We put 'emphasis on ((ends)) because the backslash ((\)) must be immediately followed by a line break. If you put a blank or any other character behind, Python will point out an error. The truth is that the bar was unnecessary. If a line ends without closing all open brackets (or braces, or brackets), you can continue on the next line.

Complete the program yourself.

Chapter 4
Control Structures

"That's why they're constantly spinning, I guess," Alice said.

"Yes, that's right," said the Hatter, "as things get dirty.

"But what happens when they return to the beginning again?" - Alice asked.

Lewis Carroll, Alice through the mirror.

The programs we have learned to build so far always have the same sequence of actions:

Data is requested from the user (assigning values obtained with raw_input to variables).

Calculations are made with the data entered by the user, saving the result in variables (through assignments).

The results stored in variables are shown on the screen (by means of the sentence print).

These programs are formed as a series of lines that are executed one after the other, from the first to the last "and following the same order in which they appear in the file: the program execution flow is strictly sequential.

However, it is possible to alter the flow of program execution to make:

make decisions based on the data and / or intermediate results and, depending on these, execute certain sentences and not others;

make decisions based on the data and / or intermediate results and, depending on these, execute certain sentences more than once.

The first type of control flow alteration is made with conditional or selection statements and the second type with iterative or repetitive sentences. The sentences that allow altering the flow of execution are included in the so-called flow control structures (which we abbreviate with the term ((control structures))).

We will study an additional way to alter the flow of control that allows us to signal, detect and treat errors that occur when executing a program: issuance sentences and exception capture.

4.1. Conditional Sentences

4.1.1. An Example Program: Solving First Degree Equations

Let's see an example. We design a program to solve any first degree equation of the form

$ax + b = 0,$

where x is the unknown.

Before we begin, we must answer two questions:

What are the problem data? (Generally, problem data will be requested from the user with raw_input.)

In our problem, the coefficients a and b are the problem data.

What do we want to calculate? (Typically, what we calculate will be shown to the user through a print statement.)

Obviously, the value of x.

Now that we know the input data and the result that we have to calculate, that is, the output data, we ask ourselves: how do we calculate the output from the input? In our example, by clearing x of the equation, we arrive at the conclusion that x is obtained by calculating –b / a.

Following the scheme of the programs that we know how to do, we will proceed like this:

We will ask for the value of a and the value of b (which we will assume of floating type).

We will calculate the value of x as –b / a.

We will show the value of x on the screen.

Let's write the following program in a text file called first grade.py:

first grade.py

```
a = float (raw_input ('Value of a:'))
b = float (raw_input ('Value of b:'))
x = -b / a
print 'Solution:', x
```

The lines are executed in the same order as they appear in the program. Let's see it work:

Value of a: 10

Value of b: 2

Solution: -0.2

To the extent possible, we must try to avoid runtime errors: they stop the execution of the program and display error messages that are not understandable to the user of the program. If in writing the program, we have provided a solution for any possible execution error, we can (and should) take control of the situation at all times.

Execution Errors

We have said that program errors that occur at runtime should be avoided and, certainly, the software development industry makes a great effort to ensure that its products are free from runtime errors. However, the large size of the programs and their complexity (coupled with the rush to bring products to market) make many of these mistakes end up being present. We have all suffered the experience of, executing an application, obtaining an error message indicating that the execution of the program has been aborted or, worse still, the computer has remained ((hung up)). If the application contained important work data and we had not saved it to disk, these would have been irretrievably lost. There is nothing more irritating to the user than an unstable application, that is, prone to the commission of errors at runtime.

The operating system is also software and is subject to the same software development problems as conventional applications. However, errors in the operating system are, as a rule, more serious, as these are usually those that leave ((hung)) the computer.

The famous ((salt and reenters the application)) or ((restarts the computer)) usually proposed as practice solution and many of these problems are a result of low levels of good quality to part of the software that is marketed.

4.1.2. The if conditional statement

In our example program we would like to detect if a zero is worth so that, in that case, we will not perform the calculation of the fourth line of the first degree.py, which is what causes the error. How to make a certain part of the program run or stop doing so based on a certain condition?

Conventional programming languages have a special sentence whose meaning is:

((At this point, execute this action (s) only if this condition is true.))

This type of statement is called conditional or selection and in Python, it is as follows:

if condition:

action

In our case, we want to detect the condition ((not worth 0)) and, only in that case, execute the last lines of the program:

first grade.py

a = float (raw_input ('Value of e:'))

b = float (raw_input ('Value of b:'))

if a! = 0:

x= -b / a

print 'Solution:', x

Let us analyze lines 4, 5, and 6 carefully. Line 4 shows the conditional statement if followed by what, as we have said, must be a condition. The condition is easily read if we know that! = Means ((is different from)). Thus, line 4 reads ((if a is other than 0)). The line that starts with if must end with a colon (:). Notice that the next two lines are written more to the right. To highlight this feature, we have drawn two vertical lines that mark the level at which the if appeared. We say that this line has more indentation or bleeding than the line that starts with if. This greater indentation indicates that the execution of these two lines depends on satisfying the condition a! = 0: only when this is true are the lines of greatest bleeding executed. Thus, when it is worth 0, those lines will not be executed, thus avoiding the error of division by zero.

Let's see what happens now if we re-enter the data that previously caused the error:

Value of a: 0

Value of b: 3

MMM. . . Nothing happens. An error does not occur, it is true, but the program ends up without providing any information. Let's analyze the cause. The first two lines of the program have been executed (we are asked for the values of a and b); the third one is blank; the fourth line has also been executed, but since the condition has not been fulfilled (worth 0), lines 5 and 6 have been ignored and as there are no more lines in the program, the execution has finished without more. An error has not occurred, of course, but ending the execution of the program can be somewhat confusing for the user. Let's see what this other program does:

first grade.py

```
a = float (raw_input ('Value of a:'))
b = float (raw_input ('Value of b:'))
if a! = 0: 5 x = -b / a
print 'Solution:', x
if a == 0:
print 'The equation has no solution.'
```

Lines 7 and 8 begin, again, with a conditional sentence. Instead of! =, The comparison operator used is ==. The sentence is read ((if a equals 0)).

As much as the student reads the program, he finds no fault. He says that line 7, which is marked as erroneous, reads like this: ((if a is equal to zero...)) Are you correct? Why is an error detected?

Running the program with the same data, we now have:

Value of a: 0

Value of b: 3

The equation has no solution.

But, given data such that a is different from 0, the program solves the equation:

Value of a: 1

Value of b: -1

Solution: 1

Let us study carefully what has happened in each case:

a = 0 and b = 3

a = 1 and b = −1

Lines 1 and 2 are executed, so that

they read the values of a and b.

Line 4 is executed and the result of the

Comparison is false. Or.

Comparison is true.

Lines 5 and 6 are ignored.

Lines 5 and 6 are executed, so that shows the solution value on

the screen of the equation: Solution: 1.

Line 7 is executed and the result.

Line 7 is executed and the result.

Comparison is true.

Comparison is false.

Line 8 is executed and displayed by pan.

Line 8 is ignored.

size the message ((The equation does not have any solution.

This type of analysis, in which we follow the course of the line-line program for a given configuration of the input data, is called the execution trace. The execution traces are very helpful in understanding what a program is doing and thus locating possible errors.

The dictionary of the Royal Academy defines electronic computer as an electronic, analog or digital machine, equipped with a large capacity memory and methods of information processing, capable of solving mathematical and logical problems through the automatic use of computer programs.

The definition itself gives us indications about some basic elements of the computer: the memory, and some device capable of performing mathematical and logical calculations.

Memory is a great store of information. In memory we store all types of data: numerical values, texts, images, etc. The device responsible for carrying out mathematical and logical operations, which is called the Arithmetic-Logic Unit (UAL), is like a calculator capable of working with that data and producing, from them, new data (the result of operations). Another device is responsible for transporting the information from the memory to the UAL, controlling the UAL to carry out the pertinent operations and depositing the results in the memory: the Control Unit. The set formed by the Control Unit and the UAL is known as the Central Processing Unit (or CPU).

We can imagine the memory as a huge closet with numbered drawers and the CPU as a person who, equipped with a calculator (the UAL), is able to search operands in memory, perform calculations with them and leave the results in memory.

Conclusion

Thank you for making it through to the end of *Python Programming Language For Beginners*, let's hope it was informative and able to provide you with all of the tools you need to achieve your goals whatever they may be.

Language has undergone an evolution since its design in the 1970s. For example, the C Language, as conceived by its authors, Brian Kernighan, and Dennis Ritchie, of the North American telecommunication company AT&T, is popularly known as K&R C and is practically obsolete. In the 1980s, C was modified and standardized by the American National Standards Institute (ANSI), which resulted in the so-called ANSI C and is now known as C89 for the year in which it was published. The standard was revised in the 90s and new features were incorporated that significantly improve the language. The result is the second edition of ANSI C, more known as C99. This is the version we will study in this course.

In this book, we have used a free C compiler: the gcc in its version 3.2 or higher. Initially, gcc was named as taking the acronym for GNU C Compiler. GNU is the name of a project that aims to offer an operating system ((free)) and all the tools that it is common to find on a Unix platform. Today, the GNU / Linux platform, which is composed of a core operating system of the Unix family (Linux) and numerous tools developed as part of the GNU project, including gcc, has become very popular. The version of gcc that we will use does not support even all the features of C99, but only those that we will learn in the course.

Any recent distribution of Linux 5 incorporates the version of gcc that we will use or higher. You can download a version of gcc and the associated utilities for Microsoft Windows at http://www.delorie.com/djgpp. On page http://www.bloodshed.net/devcpp.html you will find an integrated environment (text editor, code debugger, compiler, etc.) that also uses the gcc compiler.

Be careful, not all compilers support some features of the latest version of C, so you may experience a compatibility problem if you use a different compiler than the one we recommend.

By the same Author

PYTHON FOR DATA ANALYSIS

A Beginner's guide to wrangling and analyzing data using Python

©2019

(Clark Wes)

www.ingramcontent.com/pod-product-compliance
Lightning Source LLC
Chambersburg PA
CBHW071129050326
40690CB00008B/1392